SOCIETY OF ILLUSTRATORS
ILLUSTRATORS 23
THE TWENTY THIRD ANNUAL
OF AMERICAN ILLUSTRATION

EXHIBITION HELD IN THE GALLERIES OF THE SOCIETY OF ILLUSTRATORS
MUSEUM OF AMERICAN ILLUSTRATION, 128 EAST 63RD STREET, NEW YORK
FEBRUARY 4 — APRIL 8, 1981

SOCIETY OF ILLUSTRATORS, INC., PUBLISHERS
128 EAST 63RD STREET, NEW YORK, N.Y. 10021

ISBN-8038-3435-7
Library of Congress Catalog Card Number 59-10849

Printed and bound in Tokyo, Japan by Dai Nippon Printing Co. Ltd.

United States Distributor
Hastings House, Publishers, Inc. 10 East 40th Street, New York, N.Y. 10016

International Distributors
CANADA: Saunders of Toronto, Ltd. Markham, Ontario L3R25e
FRANCE: Graphis Distribution, Milton-La-Chapelle, F-78470 St.-Remy-Les Chevreuse
SWITZERLAND, FEDERAL REPUBLIC OF GERMANY AND AUSTRIA: Arthur Niggli, Ltd., Publishers,
    CH-9052 Niederteufen, Switzerland.
UNITED KINGDOM: Transatlantic Book Service Ltd., 24 Red Lion Street, London WCIR 4 PX
    England.
OTHER EUROPEAN COUNTRIES: Fleetbooks, c/o Feffer & Simons, B.V.Rijnkade 170 P.O. Box 112,
    1382 GT Weesp, Netherlands.
REST OF THE WORLD: Fleetbooks, c/o Feffer & Simons, 100 Park Avenue, New York, NY 10017

ROBERT HALLOCK, Designer   HOWARD MUNCE, Editor

SOCIETY OF ILLUSTRATORS
ILLUSTRATORS 23
THE TWENTY THIRD ANNUAL
OF AMERICAN ILLUSTRATION

I/23

PUBLISHED BY THE SOCIETY OF ILLUSTRATORS, INC., NEW YORK 10021
DISTRIBUTED BY HASTINGS HOUSE, PUBLISHERS, INC., NEW YORK 10016

OFFICERS (1980-1981)

Honorary President	Harold Von Schmidt
President	John Witt
Executive Vice-President	Art Weithas
Vice-President	Cal Sacks
Treasurer	Diane Dillon
Associate Treasurer	Carol Donner
Secretary	Doug Cramer
House Chairman	Gerald McConnell

ILLUSTRATORS 23 BOOK COMMITTEE

Produced for the Society by	Gerald McConnell
Production Manager	Janet Weithas
Annual Editor	Howard Munce
Annual Designer	Robert Hallock
Advertising Director	Janet Weithas

ILLUSTRATORS 23 ADVISORY BOARD

Arthur Eisman
Arie Kopelman
Gerald McConnell
Arthur Weithas
John Witt

ILLUSTRATORS 23 SHOW COMMITTEE

Poster Artist	Wilson McLean
Poster Designer	Eugene Light
Hanging Chairman	Scott Reynolds
Executive Director	Arpi Ermoyan
Show Coordinator	Terry Brown
Show Staff	Jill Bossert
	Dennis Brown
	Cathy Citarella
	Anna Lee Fuchs
	Norma Pimsler
	Janet Weithas

ILLUSTRATORS 23 JURORS

ADVERTISING
Doug Cramer, *Chairman*
Bernie D'Andrea
Leo Dillon
Joan Hall
Brad Holland
Howard E. Paine
Jack G. Tauss
John Vogler

EDITORIAL
Bernie Karlin, *Chairman*
David Attebury
Robert Deschamps
Elaine Duillo
Richard Ely
Wesley Hotchkiss
Irene Jacobusky
Jay Scott Pike

BOOK
Roland Descombes, *Chairman*
Stan Corfman
Carol Donner
Robert E. Hall
Acy Lehman
Don Ivan Punchatz
Michael Ramus
Burt Silverman

INSTITUTIONAL
Murray Tinkelman, *Chairman*
Roy Andersen
Michael Frith
Mark Hess
Don Kubly
Rick Meyerowitz
Howard Munce
Julia Noonan

TV/FILM
Tom Daly, *Chairman*
Ko Noda
Reynold Ruffins
Miriam Schottland

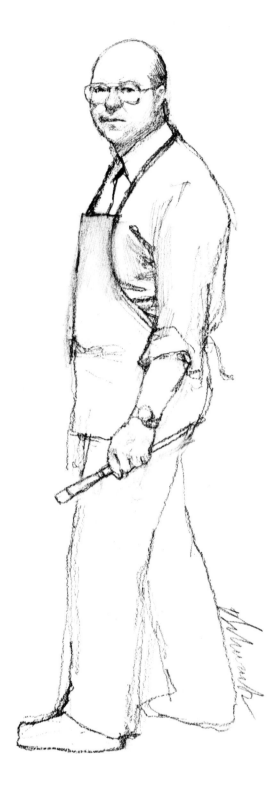

PRESIDENT'S MESSAGE

Founded in 1901, the Society of Illustrators is a public service, educational organization and museum, with a distinguished history of achievement. The recent inauguration of the S.I. Museum of American Illustration, expansion of our lecture series and student scholarship programs, and our increased interaction with other museums are visible evidence of a continuing dedication to the art of illustration and to the public we serve.

The annual exhibitions and publications also fulfill an important service, aside from exposing contemporary talent to the marketplace and to an increasingly aware public. They provide an opportunity for insightful study of our culture and history through a most unique art form.

Today's illustrators — artistic descendants of Nast, Daumier, Goya and Dürer — work in a context of freedom that earlier generations could not have imagined, and in media that reach undreamed of populations.

The burdens of truth and honesty with self, however, remain the same.

World leaders, personalities, historical and current events, the works of authors and poets are all interpreted through the illustrator's mind and hand.

This work should never be accepted casually, but rather be judged by the criteria of all art. Is the form original or imitative; is the content shallow or profound; is it false or true?

With an awareness of all these resonances, with *Illustrators 23*, we submit for your judgement another chapter of our culture, our society by illustrators.

— *John Witt*

After 21 years as Art Director of Sports Illustrated, _Dick Gangel has retired at an early age to devote time to his own painting._

He leaves a matchless record: one achieved by unwavering standards, brilliant, often daring casting of artist to assignment and a ceaseless search for exceptional talent.

And there was always the relentless pressure of producing a weekly news-oriented magazine with its murderous deadlines.

A perusal of the multitudinous issues directed by him during his brilliant tenure would reveal some of the most exciting examples of the art of illustration ever produced. Bravo!

— Editor

SUMMER MEMORIES by Richard Gangel

Looking back at the pursuit of elusive images of life in sport for the last two decades, I feel good about the venture. I can smile about the failures, and smile about the successes. It was fun and absurd, important and trivial, and it produced intriguing hand-made pictures of high quality.

The important part of the venture was involving the artist as a reporter, a reporter of visual language. He packed his bags, pencils, sketchbook and, armed with a press pass, saw firsthand what was happening. The images were based on his own experiences. The serious artist-observer gave us a deep and beautiful experience; the funny men, delicious satire.

And the stories about the artist at work! French artist André Francois appearing in my office a day or two earlier than expected and being hustled over to Madison Square Garden to see a hockey game. He disappeared for a week or so and in his hotel room painted those memorable hockey players with tiny heads and huge pads guarding the goal.

How many ways can one see Baseball's Spring Training ritual? Ronald Searle's view of the L.A. Dodgers riding bicycles in full uniform to the practice field in Palm Springs. The contrast between Bob Weaver's powerful painting-drawings of the players and spectators and the fresh sun-drenched watercolors of Jim McMullin. What can one say about Arnold Roth's madcap vision of wary groundkeeper and impudent alligator? Bernie Fuchs' report, heralding the coming of a new season, will be delivered to someone else — thin oil wash on Belgian linen, still smelling of turpentine, ready to be unrolled for that first look.

Can I ever forget those "Golden Age of Illustration" Hall of Famers Austin Briggs and Al Parker? Austin's booming voice as he delivered his Elk Hunt paintings, and the arrival of Al's magnificent pieces of the Grand Prix at Monaco. I can see us now, walking the course together, ogling the cars, boats and bottoms.

One of the joys of editorial art direction is joining the artist in an adventure. I had returned to flying, and Stanley Meltzoff and I took a Beech Baron to Providenciales in the British West Indies to search out the fighting bonefish. Meltzoff produced a stunning underwater report. Bob Peak and I walked the Masta Kink, Belgium, Nürbergring, Germany, and the Curva Grande, Monza, Italy to get research for his Most Dangerous Curves in Racing portfolio. Peak was an obsessed man, working in his cluttered warehouse space along Westport's Saugatuck River, making hundreds of drawings and studies to satisfy his personal vision.

There were dozens of riveting images ... Saul Steinberg's elegant black race horse being stared down by a tough little jockey. Bob Heindel's lonely defeated basketball player; James Rosenquist's Daytona depiction of a pat of butter skidding on a hot frying pan; Tom Allen's Remington sketchbook; Wilson McLean's portrait of Knute Rockne; Wayne Thiebaud's white tennis ball glowing on the grass at Wimbleton ... I must end this trip down memory lane without being able to mention the names and accomplishments of so many gifted illustrators.

Where is Illustration headed in the years to come? What will it be like as we turn into a new century? I feel certain that magazines will not be the same. I hope that there will still be handsome graphic presentation on paper, and a desire for fine writing.

With the reality of cable television, magazines might become plastic containers for videotape pictures with a sound track. Or they might come into the home via teleprinter. No matter, Illustration must understand the change and create a place for itself. In any case, change can not dim the timeless quest of the artist — to reveal the world as he sees it to a grateful, delighted audience.

Austin Briggs

EDITOR'S STATEMENT

Three of the first rewards that this Annual has to offer are examples of work by Hall of Fame winners F.R. Gruger, John Gannam and Stan Galli.

Gruger flourished between 1890's and 1940's. Gannam between 1920's and 1960's. Galli's brilliant output continues.

The work of each is both traditional and innovative — traditional because of its naturalistic approach, and innovative because each used his abundant talent and unique point of view to press past what others did in similar veins.

Of the three, only Galli has lived to witness the upheavals that have occurred in illustration in recent years — both in media and in direction. The bulk of this book represents, in the main, the latest of that revolutionary spirit.

It's for you to match, compare, debate and analyze the mix of minds, imaginations and beliefs that motivate the extraordinary skills of the artists represented here. Whose work does what to you? It's to be hoped that *everything* has an effect — even if it strengthens a negative opinion.

It's ironic to note that as illustration has broken all barriers in recent years, the desire to collect old works has mushroomed. (Is the reason not that bizarre for bizarre-sake winds up as preciousness without content? And does it not prove that solid creative people, no matter how wild, never lose sight of the source — which is the human figure and the earth upon which it functions?)

No longer are old illustrations blithely donated to church fairs and bazaars to be raffled off for peanuts. And no longer are the crowded bins of art departments carelessly disposed of.

What has survived of the vast output that once filled the magazine, advertising and book market now make their way into galleries and auction houses to be sold for amazing sums. Or they're welcomed into museums, notably the New Britain Museum of American Art in Connecticut and the Brandywine and Delaware Art Museum, to become part of very popular collections. Often they prompt satisfied viewers to ask what the difference is between Art and Illustration. Many others land in the happy hands of private collectors — often other illustrators.

Any reader old enough to have worked around commercial art in any capacity during the time that used illustrations were regarded so cheaply, will flinch to be reminded of the ones that passed through their hands without a thought of preservation.

The loss of such great stuff is sadly lamented — but it's nice to know that it won't happen again.

— Howard Munce

Self Portrait

DESIGNER'S COMMENTS

These Annuals are permanent records of the best contemporary work in illustration in all categories. For twenty-three years they have documented our fluid society through its interpreters, the illustrators.

In the present electronic world we are bombarded with visual images that are so fleeting that little is left to the imagination. Here is where the personal observation of the artist is called to new significance. Daily exposure to the literal reality of TV has numbed us with its repetition and clichés. We have a deeper need for the more personal world of art — drawings, paintings, constructions and sculpture. We hunger for the antidotes to bigness, violence and conformity.

Museums are increasingly becoming refuge for the sustenance we need to contemplate the roots of reality. We are restored in reviewing the evolvement of art in history. Styles emerge, bloom and die, but we constantly seek new definitions to live by.

The Society of Illustrators permanent Museum of American Illustration helps greatly in preserving our heritage, as do these annuals.

— Robert Hallock

HALL OF FAME — F.R. GRUGER

F.R. Gruger combined those rare qualities of an innovative technique, a keen sense of design and attention to details which caused him to be referred to as an artist's artist. Arthur William Brown would say: "What I learned about illustration from him was pure gold." According to Garrett Price: "We all thought a great deal of Gruger. In art school most of us imitated him or tried to." John Falter confessed that "We were greatly influenced by him because we tried to work in his style." And Norman Rockwell, reducing praise to its simplest terms, stated plainly: "I admired him very much."

Frederic Rodrigo Gruger was born in Philadelphia on August 2, 1871. He attended the Pennsylvania Academy where he studied drawing with Thomas Anshutz and compositon under Henry Thouron. Like many of his contemporaries, Gruger became enamored with the pen-and-ink drawings of Edwin Austin Abbey, Charles Reinhart and Charles Keene, and it was with this medium that he began his career as a newspaper artist.

During the decade of the '90s his on-the-spot sketches of fires, a presidential inaugural and the America's Cup Race brought immediacy and excitement to the pages of the Philadelphia *Public Ledger.*

When George Horace Lorimer reorganized the faltering *Saturday Evening Post* in 1898, he sought out the talents of such Philadelphia illustrators as F.R. Gruger. During the next forty-five years Gruger produced over 2,700 illustrations for the *Post* alone. Between 1914 and 1920 he created more than six hundred *Post* drawings, an average of two works per issue per week over the entire six-year span. By the early 1920's, at the peak of his production, Gruger was simultaneously illustrating serialized stories for the *Post, Cosmopolitan, Harper's, Harper's Bazaar, McCall's, Hearst's International* and *Redbook.*

F.R. Gruger provided visual impact for the literary outpourings of more than four hundred authors, a veritable "Who's Who" which included Theodore Dreiser, Booth Tarkington, Bret Hart, Edith Wharton, Agatha Christie, William Faulkner, Ring Lardner, Sinclair Lewis, Irving S. Cobb, W. Somerset Maugham, Mary Roberts Rinehart, F. Scott Fitzgerald, Aldous Huxley and Irving Stone. He illustrated Edna Ferber's *Show Boat,* Stephen Vincent Benet's *The Devil and Daniel Webster* and the *Mr. Moto* series by J.P. Marquand. Perhaps his best-known drawings were those for Owen Johnson's *Stover at Yale,* which appeared in *McClure's* Magazine over an eight-month period during 1911 and '12.

Gruger's illustrations received a continuous chorus of applause from the public, art editors and authors alike. Fannie Hurst wrote him that "You *have said* in your drawings what I tried to say in 100,000 words. I am your debtor!" and C.E.

All reproductions courtesy of Bennard B. Perlman, author of "F. R. Gruger and His Circle", published by North Light; F. R. Gruger Jr., and Walt Reed, Illustration House, Westport, Connecticut

Scoggins acknowledged that Gruger's illustrations for *The House of Darkness* "interpreted almost what I saw in my own mind." But the ultimate compliment for any illustrator came to him from Walter D. Edmonds, who indicated that the persons in Gruger's artwork "are all so exactly as I tried to describe them, even the house, that I now begin to find myself looking at the drawings and taking my own descriptions from them."

A portion of Gruger's uniqueness was the fact that he never worked from the posed model or from photographs, but always creatively. He also took considerable pride in the fact that not once did he ever petition an art editor for work.

Although his earliest illustrations had been produced in pen-and-ink, the medium most closely associated with his name was the Wolff carbon pencil. Gruger would sketch a composition, then employ watercolor washes with lamp black in order to indicate the broad masses of grays and blacks. Finally he built up the forms and details with a Wolff pencil, rubbing a ruby eraser like a stump to blend the rich, velvety values.

The illustration board he employed was an inexpensive cardboard used by newspapers for mounting silverprints. Known originally as railroad blank, it soon was manufactured under his name, and Gruger Board became the mainstay of illustrators for several decades.

At the Art Students League, Thomas Fogarty would "hold Gruger up as one of the deans of beautiful illustration and storytelling," while Harold Anderson's teacher at Boston's Fenway School of Illustration "frequently called Gruger to our attention, praising him as the finest of them all." At the Art Institute of Chicago, Garrett Price's instructor "got a whole carload of that [Gruger] board shipped into Chicago." And John Falter, studying illustration at the Kansas City Art Institute, had a teacher who "held up F.R. Gruger along with Wyeth and Pyle as a giant to be aware of and study."

But by the mid-1930's Gruger's influence was on the wane. He had never bothered to make the transition from black-and-white illustrations to color but, of even greater importance, his type of pictorial approach, with its attention to detail — to facial qualities, pose, appropriateness of architectural components, furnishings and dress — was no longer in vogue. Magazine art, in imitation of the movies' favorite device, began emphasizing the big closeup; such "He and She" art featured oversized faces and little else.

Nonetheless, when *Time* Magazine included an article entitled "U.S. Illustrators" in its May 1, 1939 issue, Gruger was not forgotten: "As worthy as Gibson to be called the dean of U.S. illustrators, in the opinion of many artists, is a stolid, 68-year-old Philadelphian ..., Frederic Rodrigo Gruger." And a dozen years later, when the Society of Illustrators celebrated its 50th Anniversary with an exhibition of the "Big Four," Gruger was there along with Harvey Dunn, Wallace Morgan and Norman Price.

F.R. Gruger passed away just seventeen months after that show, on March 21, 1953. Now, exactly three decades following the Society exhibit, he finally joins the others of the "Big Four" by being inducted into the Hall of Fame.

As with all artists, Gruger's work stands as his monument. His goals were once summarized when he sought to explain his refusal to draw "those chromium-plated women":

One may perceive the charm of smart clothes and exquisite equipment, of beautiful women and well-dressed men, of trimmed hedges and smooth lawns and weedless paths ... I could never do anything with it so I left it to others and contented myself with admiration of what they did. For me the weathered street, the lived-in houses, the old trees ... Used belongings, comfortably worn and pushed about into homely order long before the incident in the story occurred. To remain, bearing the scars of use, long after it has passed.
Perhaps that is the poetry of character.

And that is also the poetry of F.R. Gruger's art.
— *Bennard B. Perlman*

Bennard B. Perlman is the author of
"The Golden Age of American Illustration F.R. GRUGER and His Circle"
Published by North Light Publishers, Westport, Connecticut, 1978.

Collier's

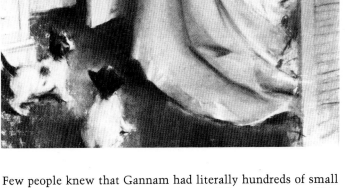

HALL OF FAME — **JOHN GANNAM**

The most difficult detective work connected with this edition was to pin down the late elusive and elfin John Gannam.

Many knew a bit about him; mostly the same bits. The one fact that everyone agreed upon was what a superb illustrator he was.

Leafing through dozens of his old tear sheets for this volume was a jolting experience. His pictures would have been splendid in any medium — the fact that they were done in watercolor with its attendant traps and difficulties make them even more amazing.

Below are three affectionate excerpts by contemporaries who shake their heads and smile at the recollection of his name, talent and spooky ways.

— *Editor*

John Gannam was the ultimate illustrator's artist. A funny-looking, baldheaded little guy, he painted beautiful women with a love and flow of sensitivity. There was never anything tricked-up, smart-alecky or hokey about John's work. One could easily think of Gannam and Sargent at the same time.

He was also an editor's and art director's nightmare, for he was never quite satisfied with his stuff. Deadlines always came second to perfection. A story set for a winter issue might be ready for a summer one. This never ruffled him and nobody ever saw anything less than what he considered his best. There are always apochyrphal stories about characters like John, and some said he seldom changed his socks. If this were true maybe the rest of us change ours too often.

When I knew him he was a third of a not-very-holy trinity composed of Dean Cornwell, Harry Beckhoff and himself, quietly brilliant, waiting in the corner with the short verbal capper. A latter-day Zorn disguised as an Armenian rug peddler. I was always pleased to be asked in as a fourth and was honored to play dummy.

My favorite story about John concerned a dinner President John Holmgren organized at the Society for Bill Chessman when he left *Collier's*. All of us who drew pictures for "Chess" were there. Gannam, noted for his beautiful women, was invariably hired by Chessman to paint horses in Westerns. After all the tearful-and-otherwise speeches had been made, our hero rose to his full five-foot-four stature and made the keynote speech of the evening: "I always thought Chessman was a sonofabitch, and I still think so!"

The Illustrators will not see the likes of John Gannam again.

— *Charles Hawes*

Few people knew that Gannam had literally hundreds of small pastels (7x10) landscapes scattered around the many rooms of his messy studio. They were exquisite. But he rarely used pastel for assignments.

One year he did a theatrical drop for a Society Girlie Show. It was a sylvan pool rendered in pastel. It was spontaneously applauded when the curtain rose.

John was evasive about how he achieved his results in any medium. I was always curious to know how he knew so much about cowboys, luxurious interiors and the variety of subjects he illustrated. His answer was, "Oh, I have friends."

— *Tran Mawicke*

Some years ago I chaired the Society's lecture series. I had Johnny scheduled one evening and he hated it. He claimed he had nothing to say. His only courage was a tumbler of straight whiskey kept just out of sight in the wings offstage. Frequently he politely excused himself, to supposedly clear his throat. His naturally quiet voice was difficult to hear in the rear; it became totally inaudible when he strayed. I finally forced him to hold onto the stand of the microphone even when he walked around. He began to lean on it, and since it was telescopic, it slowly began to get shorter with Johnny following it down, still talking. He ended up bent way down with his head about on the level with his knees and the student audience howling with glee. What his pearly words were at that time remain known only to his knees.

— *Kenneth W. Thompson*

Reader's Digest

HALL OF FAME — **STANLEY W. GALLI**

Stan Galli for many years has been a successful San Francisco illustrator whose work has appeared regularly in some of America's most prestigious popular magazines. Galli's career presents us with the near perfect western archetype that many of us of that generation aspired to. There has always been an integrity and honesty in Galli's work that both buyer and viewer can immediately recognize and accept. To survive the lean years of the 1930's west coast artists learned to work economically with directness and simplicity. This has always been true of the Galli style and it is one of his most identifiable hallmarks.

Stan Galli knew very early in his life to what purpose it must be lived. As a young boy his talent for artistic expression attracted attention. His resolve was strengthened by this recognition and the various awards it earned for him. It seemed that nothing could go wrong, but as Murphy's Law states, it could and did. Plans for a formal art education were abruptly knocked down by force of the Great Depression, and a long interruption of sustenance jobs took their place. Frying doughnuts as a baker's apprentice was one of the first, followed by the rugged life as a hired hand on a Nevada cattle ranch. After this stint came the forgettable period of sweating out the San Francisco waterfront as a longshoreman during the violent days of the dock strikes. Galli worked at whatever he could get, his sense of purpose still intact. The slogging detail of truckdriver, delivering linen supplies to flophouses and whorehouses on the night run between Fresno and San Francico, eventually gained him enough resources to make his way through the doors of the California School of Fine Arts, where his first formal art study began. The money saved, with scholarships and awards kept him there for several years, but part-time work to help him continue was soon indicatd.

It was found in one of San Francisco's best art workshops. Thrust prematurely into the professional world totally without practical experience, Galli found himself working among some of the best artists on the west coast. It was a traumatic period of frustration, struggle and hard learning among his more experienced peers, but it was the turning point in his career.

In the world of creativity, the art fraternity is perhaps unique in its generosity toward its young hopefuls, helping and guiding each promising new talent as it comes along into the mainstream almost as a given responsibility. Most influential in the development of Galli as a first-rate professional artist were Fred Ludekens, Haines Hall and Gilbert Darling, all prominent San Francisco artists active in the professional art world. Their care and interest in Galli as an artist helped greatly in the formation of what came to be the Galli style.

In California, old guards Maynard Dixon, Maurice Logan and Harold Von Schmidt were the then respected caretakers of the West Coast style. But it was a time of change, and other San Francisco-trained artists like John Atherton, Frank MacIntosh, Ludekens and Darling were looking toward the east. Von Schmidt, who was one of the first to leave San Francisco, brought the west coast tradition with him. The others took on eastern influences and were soon absorbed into the New York milieu.

These departures, admittedly opened the market for the new

generation coming up in San Francisco. Stan Galli's life became easier as he assumed a partnership in the art service. His vision widened as his interest in the open life of the west developed. His love of the wilderness and its wildlife found its way into his work.

His first great break on the national scene came from Weyerhaeuser, who commissioned him to create for the company a new image, as conservator and protector of the western wilderness and its natural resources. Galli's paintings, as part of the Weyerhaeuser program to allay and educate the public, were marvellously effective and remained a key factor in their advertising program for over fourteen years. Although New York itself had no great appeal for Stan Galli (he visited the city once in the late 1940's for a month) a regular flow of assignments started moving toward the Galli easel, now located in Kentfield, north of San Francisco.

Beyond subject matter, what are the characteristics of the Galli style that sets it apart and makes it so compellingly pleasing? Sharp focus realism and precise representation, held together by a clear color palette pushed to a surprising strength. There is also firm design in which a penetrating sense of dramatic story-telling detail is contained. One can sense always the clear line of intent that runs continuously through his work. He paints as he must, with pragmatic honesty, and is this the essence of himself that he communicates.

Adaptability and versatility are key words in the survival kit of most west coast artists. This is especially true of Stan Galli. The variety of ventures, the challenges he has met head-on, attest to his lively interest in the wider development of his work. His exploration of new areas of activity are all a part of his need to stay fresh. In the disruptive 1960's when the disillusioned young were aimlessly copping out, Galli found a need to proselytize his personal beliefs. He found the time to teach art courses at the college level on the philosophy of *effort* in art. Again, he communicated as in his art, with effective results.

In the more current present Galli has shifted the emphasis of his work from illustration to easel painting. The vanished past of Colonial Spanish California is the focus of his interest. He paints, now for himself, the old ways of the vaquero. His research is prodigious and accurate. Early California ranch society as recorded in journals and historical records of the period before the advent of Yankee influences fascinates him. A new world is being created on canvas, from one long gone, in an inspired series of paintings that have been exhibited with success in two California museums and various regional galleries.

It is fitting that we at the Society of Illustrators should cap the distinguished career of this artist as an illustrator and painter by awarding him our finest honor. His place in the Illustrators' Hall of Fame has been justly earned and properly bestowed.

— *Harry Carter*

HAMILTON KING AWARD — GERALD McCONNELL

Robert Heindel

Jerry McConnell is like a cowboy in ways more important than his opulent handlebar mustache, Levi's and snake-proof boots. It's his attitude. He's always known what he wanted and went out and got it. This is partly a result of being a child of the '30s when the work ethic was intact plus the hundreds of paperback Westerns he read and illustrated.

It is not unusual for artists to emerge from homes where there is no direct creative impetus. Jerry's father was an engineer for Bell Labs. And if Jerry had not gotten tuberculosis when he was 18, he might not have turned to illustration. While recuperating for two years in bed, boredom drove him to copy pictures in National Geographic. At the same time, a neighbor who had lost his son in the war, befriended McConnell. He took him to hear Frank Reilly lecture at a local women's club. Reilly said he could "teach a wooden Indian to draw." Jerry's response to such bravado was to join the Art Students League where he studied for five years. In his second year he began working as an illustrator. The precepts taught by Reilly — drive, incentive and work — put him in good stead. During his stint at the League, he became a go-fer and assistant to Dean Cornwell. He also got a chance to listen in on the gossip of the great illustrators who gathered at Cornwell's for cocktails. Mead Schaeffer, Arthur William Brown and John Gannam not only knew how to paint, they knew how to live; glamorously. They paid as much attention to their pleasures as to their work.

Jerry was a commercial success from the start; up through the late sixties he did over 2,000 covers, mostly Westerns. By mid-sixties, bored with the guy, gun and horse format, he wanted a change in style. Al Catalano at AT&T gave him a chance. An assignment in 1967 came with the direction: "Give me anything, but give me something different." Jerry's something different was his first assemblage, a box filled with artfully arranged buttons, coins and symbols of the convulsive society of the '60's. Assemblages need to be photographed, so he teamed with Cosimo Scianna to shoot his stuff. In turn, when Cosimo needed an impossible prop, Jerry crafted it. Over the years they have collaborated on everything from an underwater treasure chest — with a live shark! — to a wind tunnel, to 80,000 people inside a Goodyear tire, to a gallows that worked, plus the famous mummy that won them a Gold Clio.

In addition to his other abilities, Jerry is an outstanding organizational man. He joined the Society of Illustrators in 1961 and in two years was on the Board of Directors. He's been an Executive Committee member for 14 years.

He has been a prime mover in the Graphic Artists Guild. In 1976, he helped merge the new Illustrators Guild with GAG. He is now National President of the 4,000 member organization that has chapters in six cities. His Guild work has been most satisfying because it's effecting changes in the laws and art business procedures and conduct. With all this, he still loves to draw and paint for clients and for himself. Especially for himself. His Hamilton King Award winner is just such a work. It's a rendition of Grand Central Station on a scale and with the fine detail that befits such a monument.

In the midst of a killing schedule of art work, meetings, renovation on his new loft building and time for his three children, Jerry McConnell remembers to dream. As he puts it: "Illustrators are fantasy purveyors."

— Jill Bossert

ILLUSTRATORS 23   THE TWENTY THIRD ANNUAL OF AMERICAN ILLUSTRATION

1
Artist: **ETIENNE DELESSERT**
Art Director: Walter Herdeg
Magazine: Graphis
Category: Editorial
Gold Medal

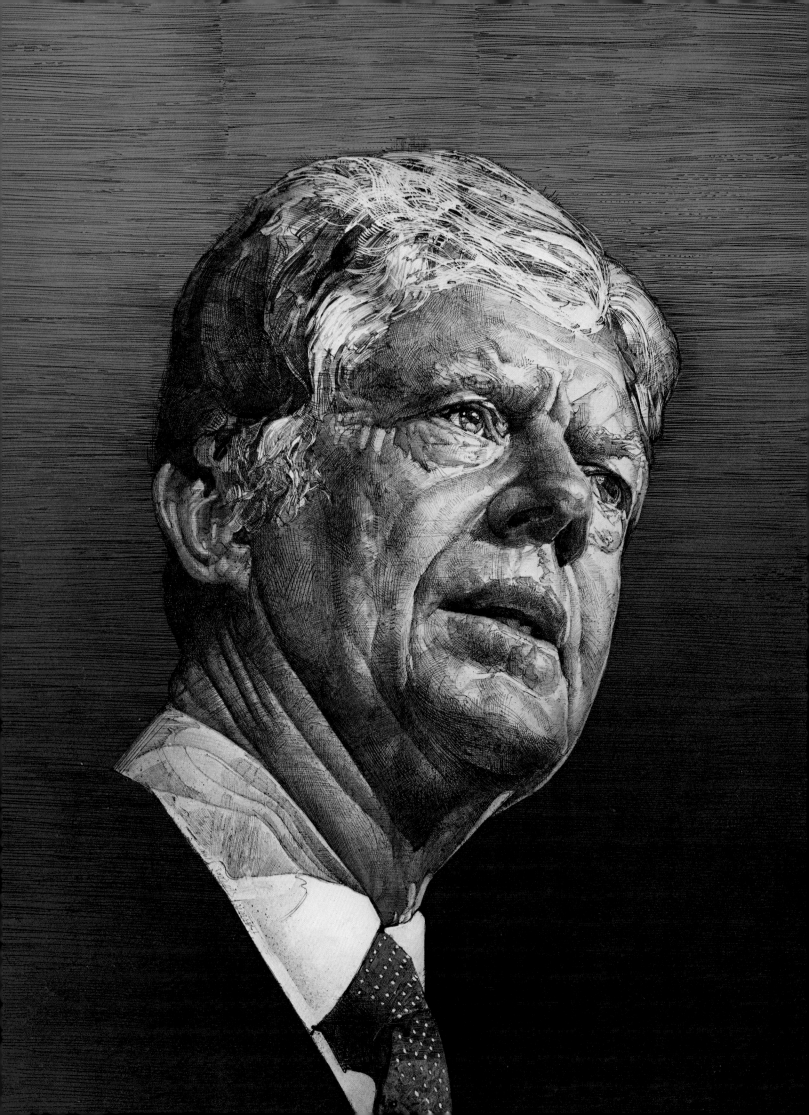

BULLETIN: AN ATTEMPT TO RESCUE THE AMERICAN HOSTAGES IN IRAN WAS ABORTED FRIDAY WHEN EIGHT CREW MEMBERS OF A U.S. AIRCRAFT WERE KILLED . . . PRESIDENT CARTER "ACCEPTS FULL RESPONSIBILITY . . . . "

3
Artist: **DANIEL SCHWARTZ**
Art Directors: Walter Bernard/Rudy Hoglund
Magazine: Time
Category: Editorial

2
Artist: **BARRON STOREY**
Art Director: Walter Bernard
Magazine: Time
Category: Editorial

4
Artist: **PHILIP BURKE**
Art Director: Noel Werrett
Magazine: Quest/80
Category: Editorial

5
Artist: **SKIP LIEPKE**
Art Directors: Walter Bernard/Rudy Hoglund
Magazine: Time
Category: Editorial

6
Artist: **JON McINTOSH**
Category: Editorial

7
Artist: **ROBERT GROSSMAN**
Art Director: John Berg
Client: CBS Records
Category: Advertising

8
Artist: **DAVID GROVE**
Art Director: David Boss
Client: NFL Properties
Category: Institutional

9
Artist: **DAVID LEVINE**
Art Director: Rudy Hoglund
Magazine: Time
Category: Editorial

10
Artist: **JIM CAMPBELL**
Art Director: Stanley Braverman
Magazine: Signature
Category: Editorial

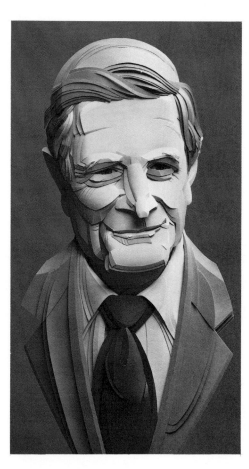

11
Artist: **RAY AMEIJIDE**
Art Director: Leonard Wolfe
Magazine: Fortune
Category: Editorial

12
Artist: **SAM VIVIANO**
Art Director: Noel Werrett
Magazine: Quest/80
Category: Editorial

13
Artist: **BURT SILVERMAN**
Art Director: Leonard Wolfe
Magazine: Fortune
Category: Editorial

14
Artist: **BOB CROFUT**
Art Director: Richard Carter
Publisher: Easton Press
Category: Book

15
Artist: **TONY SELLA**
Category: Editorial

16
Artist: **WILLIAM ERSLAND**
Art Director: Tom Roper
Client: Cliff's Notes
Category: Advertising

17
Artist: **HODGES SOILEAU**
Art Director: Richard Carter
Publisher: Easton Press
Category: Book

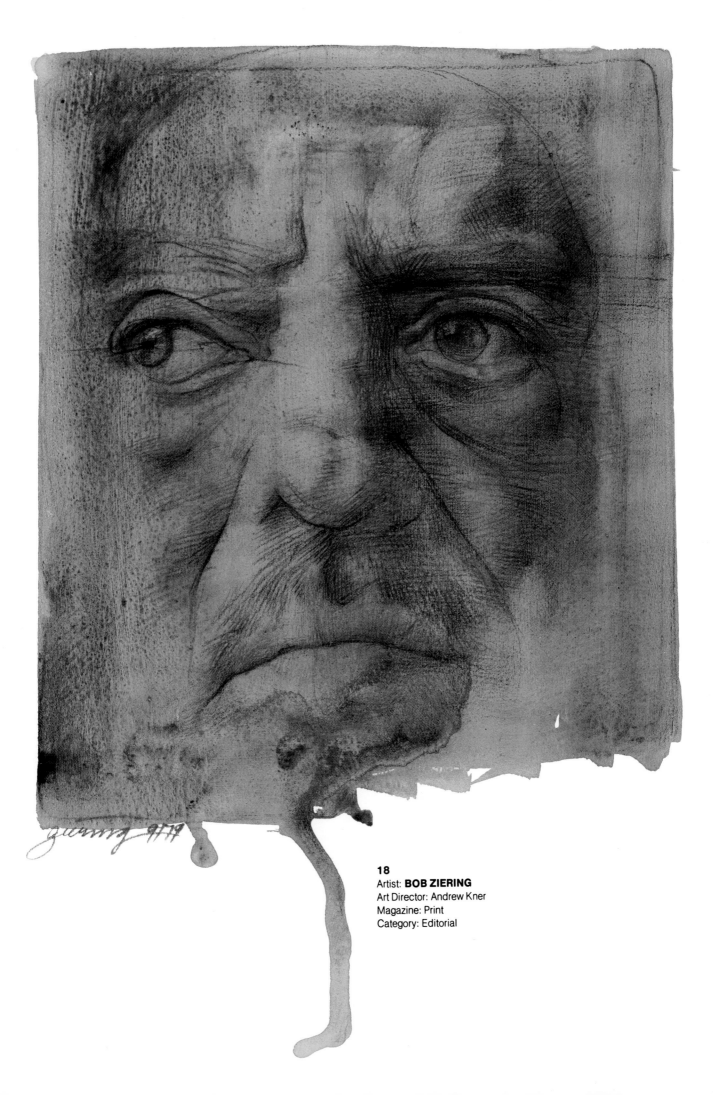

18
Artist: **BOB ZIERING**
Art Director: Andrew Kner
Magazine: Print
Category: Editorial

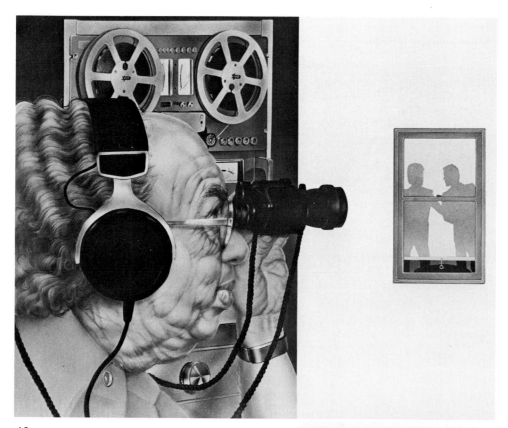

19
Artist: **JOANN DALEY**
Art Director: Jim Chada
Magazine: Hustler
Category: Editorial

20
Artist: **R.J. SHAY**
Category: Institutional

21
Artist: **RICHARD HESS**
Art Director: Susan Lyster
Agency: McCaffrey & McCall
Client: Exxon Corporation
Category: Advertising

22
Artist: **GEORGE ANGELINI**
Art Director: Dolores Gudzin
Client: NBC
Category: Television

23
Artist: **RICHARD SPARKS**
Art Director: Richard Carter
Publisher: Easton Press
Category: Book

24
Artist: **JIM CAMPBELL**
Art Director: Richard Carter
Publisher: Easton Press
Category: Book

25
Artist: **AMY WAX**
Category: Advertising

26
Artist: **BOB PEAK**
Art Director: Carl Leick
Client: Western Airlines
Category: Advertising

27
Artist: **RICHARD SPARKS**
Art Director: Richard Carter
Publisher: Easton Press
Category: Book

28
Artist: **J. MICHAEL SPOONER**
Category: Institutional

29
Artist: **HOWARD KOSLOW**
Art Director: W.K. Plummer
Client: Franklin Philatelic Society
Category: Institutional

30
Artist: **GARY KELLEY**
Client: Hellman Design Associates
Category: Advertising

31
Artist: **DANIEL MAFFIA**
Art Director: Louise Fili
Publisher: Pantheon Books
Category: Book

32
Artist: **SHARON KNETTELL**
Category: Editorial

33
Artist: **KYE CARBONE**
Category: Institutional

34
Artist: **ROBERT J. STEELE**
Category: Editorial

35
Artist: **JIM PROKELL**
Category: Editorial

36
Artist: **GERRY GERSTEN**
Art Director:Robert Hallock
Client: Society of Illustrators
Category: Book

37
Artist: **GERRY GERSTEN**
Art Director: Robert Hallock
Client: Society of Illustrators
Category: Book

38
Artist: **ED RENFRO**
Client: American Artists
Category: Institutional

39
Artist: **GERRY GERSTEN**
Art Director: Philip Growick
Client: Industrial Education
Category: Advertising

40
Artist: **GERRY GERSTEN**
Art Director: Philip Growick
Client: Industrial Education
Category: Advertising

41
Artist: **GERRY GERSTEN**
Art Director: Philip Growick
Client: Industrial Education
Category: Advertising

42
Artist: **DENNIS CORRIGAN**
Agency: Corrigan Advertising
Client: Quaker Stove Co.
Category: Advertising

43
Artist: **DENNIS CORRIGAN**
Agency: Corrigan Advertising
Client: Quaker Stove Co.
Category: Television

44
Artists: **MARILYN BASS/MARVIN GOLDMAN**
Art Director: Stanley Wheatman
Publisher: Reader's Digest Educational Division
Category: Book

45
Artist: **JOAN STEINER**
Art Director: Tom Clemente
Client: Newspaper Advertising Bureau
Category: Advertising

46
Artist: **WILLIAM ERSLAND**
Art Director: Janet Welch
Client: Northwestern Bell
Category: Advertising

47
Artist: **DAVID NOYES**
Category: Advertising

48
Artist: **MICHAEL KATZ**
Art Director: Lee Strausland
Client: The Today Show
Category: Television

49
Artist: **RICK TULKA**
Category: Editorial

50
Artist: **JOHN DE AMICIS**
Category: Institutional

51
Artist: **EDWARD SOREL**
Art Director: Robert Priest
Magazine: Esquire
Category: Editorial

A Collection Of Cold-Nosed
Consorts Cavort In Dynamic
Doggy Diversions

Hilarious Harlequins Hatch Hijinks
Of Happy Mirth-Making Mayhem

Proudly Presented By Persevering Professional Printers   Lovingly Labored And Lavishly Lithographed By Virginia Lithograph

Treacherous Tangle Of Tigers
Features Fantastic Feline Frills

Washington DC

52
Artist: **MICHAEL DAVID BROWN**
Art Directors: Michael David Brown/Jeanne Krohn
Client: Internal Revenue Service
Category: Institutional

53
Artist: **MICHAEL DAVID BROWN**
Art Directors: Michael David Brown/Jeanne Krohn
Client: Virginia Lithograph
Category: Institutional

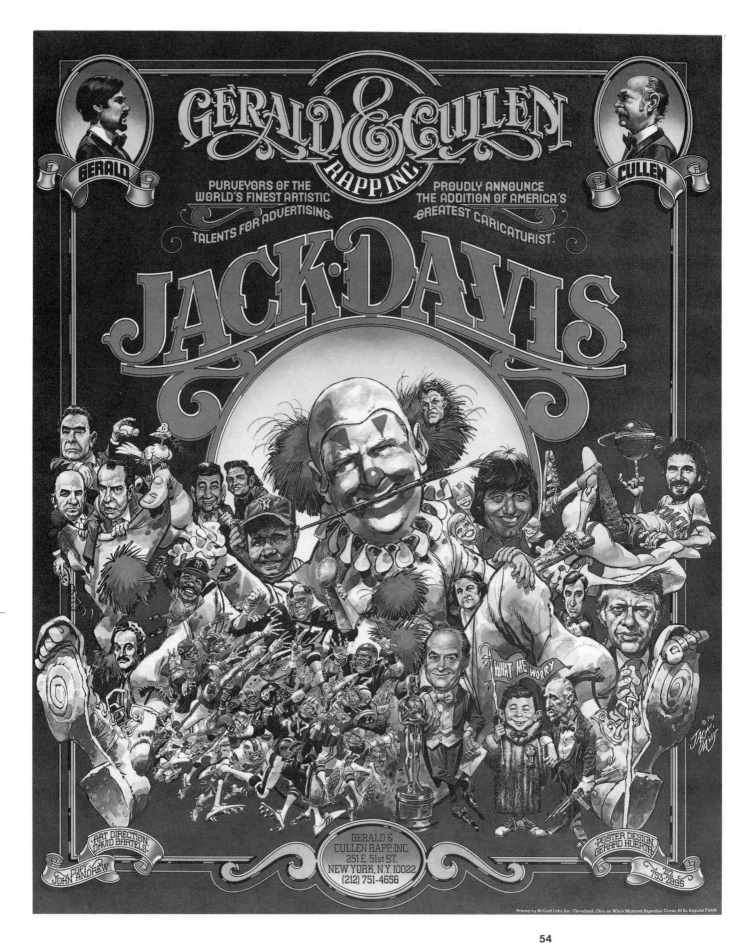

54
Artists: **JACK DAVIS/GERARD HUERTA**
Art Director: David Bartels
Client: Gerald & Cullen Rapp
Category: Institutional

55
Artist: **DENNIS CORRIGAN**
Category: Institutional

56
Artist: **DEE D'ANDREA**
Art Director: Mike Mohamad
TV Director: Bill Feigenbaum
Company: Feigenbaum Productions, Inc.
Client: NBC-TV
Category: TV

57
Artist: **ROY ANDERSEN**
Art Director: Walter Bernard
Magazine: Time
Category: Editorial

58
Artist: **THOMAS INGHAM**
Art Directors: Tom Staebler/Len Willis
Magazine: Playboy
Category: Editorial
Gold Medal

59
Artist: **PETER FIORE**
Category: Advertising

60
Artist: **LUCINDA COWELL**
Art Director: Louise Kollenbaum
Magazine: Mother Jones
Category: Editorial

SKETCHPAD STUDIO © 1980

61
Artist: **CHAD DRAPER**
Art Director: Don Punchatz
Client: Sketchpad Studio
Category: Institutional

62
Artist: **BRAD HOLLAND**
Art Director: Steve Heller
Client: A.I.G.A.
Category: Advertising

63
Artist: **JULIE SHENKMAN**
Art Director: Bob Paganucci
Client: Ciba-Geigy
Category: Institutional

64
Artist: **STEVE KARCHIN**
Art Director: Vince Maiello
Client: Playboy Book Club
Category: Advertising

65
Artist: **BRAD HOLLAND**
Art Directors: Tom Staebler/Kerig Pope
Magazine: Playboy
Category: Editorial

66
Artist: **TOM CURRY**
Art Director: Greg Paul
Publication: The Cleveland Plain Dealer Magazine
Category: Editorial

67
Artist: **GERALD McCONNELL**
Category: Book
Hamilton King Award

68
Artist: **LARRY A. GERBER**
Category: Institutional

70
Artist: **DENNIS LYALL**
Art Director: Vince Maiello
Client: Playboy Book Club
Category: Advertising

69
Artist: **JEREMY ROSS**
Art Director: Jeremy Ross
Client: Katherine Tise
Category: Institutional

71
Artist: **STEVEN GUARNACCIA**
Art Director: Italo Lupi
Magazine: Abitare
Category: Editorial

72
Artist: **STEVEN GUARNACCIA**
Art Director: Carol Carson
Magazine: Scholastic
Category: Editorial

73
Artist: **RICHARD WILLIAMS**
Category: Institutional

74
Artist: **RANDALL ENOS**
Art Director: Andrew Kner
Client: The New York Times
Category: Advertising

75
Artist: **JUDI MINTZER**
Art Directors: Dale Moyer/Jeff Direcki
Magazine: Scholastic
Category: Editorial

76
Artist: **MICHAEL GARLAND**
Art Director: Ellen Lo Guidice
Publisher: Beaufort Books
Category: Book

77
Artist: **VINCENT DZIERSKI**
Category: Institutional

78
Artist: **JEFF PIENKOS**
Client: Abbott Laboratories
Category: Institutional

79
Artist: **STEVEN H. STROUD**
Category: Editorial

80
Artist: **HODGES SOILEAU**
Art Directors: Jack Ehn/Athena Blackorby
Publisher: Harcourt Brace Jovanovich
Category: Book

81
Artist: **MEL WILLIGES**
Category: Institutional

82
Artist: **HERB TAUSS**
Art Director: Salvatore Lazzarotti
Magazine: Guideposts
Category: Editorial

83
Artist: **KENNETH FRANCIS DEWEY**
Art Director: Jack Tauss
Publisher: The Franklin Library
Category: Book

84
Artist: **STEPHEN CHARLES DE SANTO**
Category: Book

85
Artist: **LARRY WINBORG**
Category: Editorial

86
Artist: **KENNETH HOBSON**
Category: Institutional

87
Artist: **RICHARD HESS**
Art Director: Len Sirowitz
Agency: Rosenfeld. Sirowitz & Lawson
Category: Advertising

88
Artist: **DAVID GAMBALE**
Art Director: Steve Byram
Client: Ambition Records
Category: Advertising

89
Artist: **SKIP LIEPKE**
Category: Editorial

90
Artist: **SKIP LIEPKE**
Category: Editorial

91
Artist: **MAX GINSBURG**
Client: Harbor Gallery
Category: Institutional

92
Artist: **MAX GINSBURG**
Client: Harbor Gallery
Category: Institutional

93
Artist: **RICK McCOLLUM**
Art Director: Herb Bleiweiss
Client: Artists Associates
Category: Institutional

94
Artist: **RICK McCOLLUM**
Art Director: William Gregory
Publisher: Reader's Digest
Category: Book

95
Artist: **ERIC FOWLER**
Category: Book

96
Artist: **DAVID BLOSSOM**
Art Director: William Gregory
Publisher: Reader's Digest
Category: Book

97
Artist: **ANDREA MISTRETTA**
Client: Unlimited Possibilities
Category: Institutional

98
Artist: **TED LEWIN**
Art Director: Robert Grant
Publisher: Reader's Digest General Books
Category: Book

99
Artist: **JACQUI MORGAN**
Art Director: Rainer Wortmann
Magazine: Playboy Germany
Category: Editorial

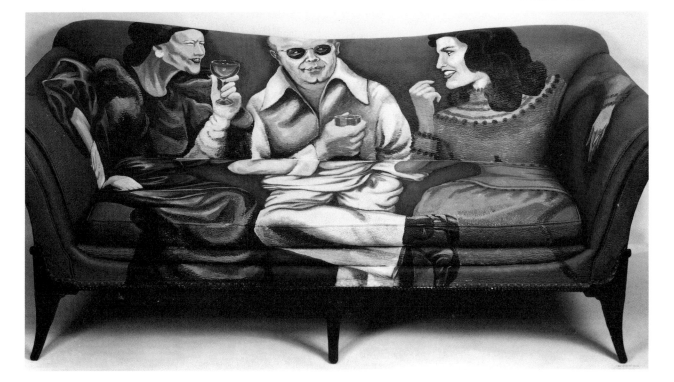

THE LUCKY WATCH

"Your arm's as good as new. See, not even a scar," Doctor Cable said to Julie when he removed the cast from her arm.

Even then Julie looked at me doubtfully before she inspected her arm, taking care to flick off any stubborn flecks of plaster dust that still adhered before she solemnly agreed. As she skipped happily ahead to the waiting room, Doctor Cable turned to me and said with a grin, "Thought she was going to demand a second opinion there for a minute."

That was three weeks ago. Now as I sat watching winged seed pods of maple leaves glance off the windshield, waiting for Julie to gather up her school books, I wondered if there was a scar after all—invisible, but there all the same.

Normally on a blue and gold day like today, Julie wouldn't miss riding her bike to school, but ever since she'd fallen on the way home one afternoon and broken her arm, the shiny *(continued)*

What is the secret of overcoming fear and gaining confidence? A mother and daughter both find out, and learn that love is essential, too. A short story by Madeleine Costigan.

Illustration by Sharon Knettell

101
Artist: **TERESA WOODWARD**
Category: Editorial

100
Artist: **SHARON KNETTELL**
Art Director: Don Adamec
Magazine: Ladies Home Journal
Category: Editorial

102
Artist: **JERRY PINKNEY**
Art Director: Roz Barden
Magazine: Redbook
Category: Editorial

103
Artist: **LLOYD BLOOM**
Art Director: Alan Benjamin
Publisher: Macmillian Publishing Co.
Category: Book

104
Artist: **LLOYD BLOOM**
Art Director: Alan Benjamin
Publisher: Macmillian Publishing Co.
Category: Book

105
Artist: **JEFF SEAVER**
Art Director: Thomas Darnsteadt
Magazine: Diagnosis
Category: Editorial

106
Artist: **MICHAEL DUDASH**
Art Director: Salvatore Lazzarotti
Magazine: Guideposts
Category: Editorial

107
Artist: **JAMES McMULLAN**
Art Director: Richard Gangel
Magazine: Sports Illustrated
Category: Editorial

108
Artist: **BOB CROFUT**
Art Director: Salavatore Lazzarotti
Magazine: Guideposts
Category: Editorial

109
Artist: **RICK McCOLLUM**
Art Directors: Jack Ehn/Athena Blackorby
Publisher: Harcourt Brace Jovanovich
Category: Book

110
Artist: **NORM WALKER**
Art Director: Barbara Bertoli
Publisher: Avon/Camelot
Category: Book

111
Artist: **TOM HALL**
Art Director: William Gregory
Publisher: Reader's Digest
Category: Book

112
Artist: **HARVEY DINNERSTEIN**
Client: FAR Gallery
Category: Institutional

113
Artist: **YALE FACTOR**
Category: Book

115
Artist: **ARTHUR SHILSTONE**
Art Director: Reg Massie
Magazine: Gourmet
Category: Editorial

116
Artist: **BERNIE FUCHS**
Art Directors: Ken Ellis/Marion Davis
Publisher: Reader's Digest
Category: Book

114
Artist: **BART FORBES**
Category: Institutional

117
Artist: **MICHAEL DUDASH**
Art Director: Bruce Hall
Publisher: Dell Publishing Co.
Category: Book

118
Artist: **JOHN THOMPSON**
Art Director: Marion Davis
Publisher: Reader's Digest
Category: Book

119
Artist: **GORDON JOHNSON**
Art Directors: Gerald Counihan/Gerald Pfeifer
Publisher: Fawcett Books
Category: Book

120
Artist: **MILT KOBAYASHI**
Art Director: Salvatore Lazzarotti
Magazine: Guideposts
Category: Editorial

121
Artist: **MICHAEL DUDASH**
Art Director: Marion Davis
Publisher: Reader's Digest
Category: Book

122
Artist: **MICHAEL DUDASH**
Art Director: Marion Davis
Publisher: Reader's Digest
Category: Book

123
Artist: **ROBERT HEINDEL**
Art Director: Reagan Wilson
Client: American Illustrators Gallery
Category: Institutional
Special Past Chairmen's Committee Award

124
Artist: **THEA KLIROS**
Art Directors: Ina Kahn/Vic Leibert
Client: Centennial Textiles
Category: Advertising

125
Artist: **THEA KLIROS**
Art Directors: Ina Kahn/Vic Leibert
Client: Pressman-Gutman
Category: Advertising

126
Artist: **BOB ZIERING**
Art Director: Janet Ferguson
Agency: Tracy Locke Advertising
Client: Haggar Slacks
Category: Advertising

127
Artist: **MEL ODOM**
Art Directors: Tom Staebler/Kerig Pope
Magazine: Playboy
Category: Editorial
Award of Excellence

128
Artist: **MEL ODOM**
Art Directors: Tom Staebler/Kerig Pope
Magazine: Playboy
Category: Editorial

130
Artist: **BART FORBES**
Art Director: Tina Adamek
Magazine: Post Graduate Medicine
Category: Editorial

129
Artist: **DENNIS LUZAK**
Art Directors: Herb Bleiweiss/Bruce Danbrot
Magazine: Good Housekeeping
Category: Editorial

131
Artist: **JOSEPH CIARDIELLO**
Art Director: Susan Lyster
Agency: McCaffery & McCall
Client: Exxon Corporation
Category: Advertising

132
Artist: **IVAN CHERMAYEFF**
Agency: Chermayeff & Geismar
Client: Mobil Corporation
Category: Advertising

133
Artist: **KIRSTEN SODERLIND**
Art Director: Frank Devito
Agency: Young & Rubicam
Client: André Champagne
Category: Advertising

134
Artist: **GILLIAN HILLS**
Art Director: Milton Charles
Publisher: Pocket Books
Category: Book

135
Artist: **HEATHER COOPER**
Art Director: Peter Nevraumont
Client: Ruby Street
Category: Institutional

136
Artist: **JACK UNRUH**
Art Director: Mauriesio Arias
Agency: Sarraille & Poole
Client: Adolphus Hotel
Category: Advertising

137
Artist: **LISA ADAMS**
Art Directors: Michael Wolk/Mimi Stein
Client: CBS Disco International
Category: Advertising

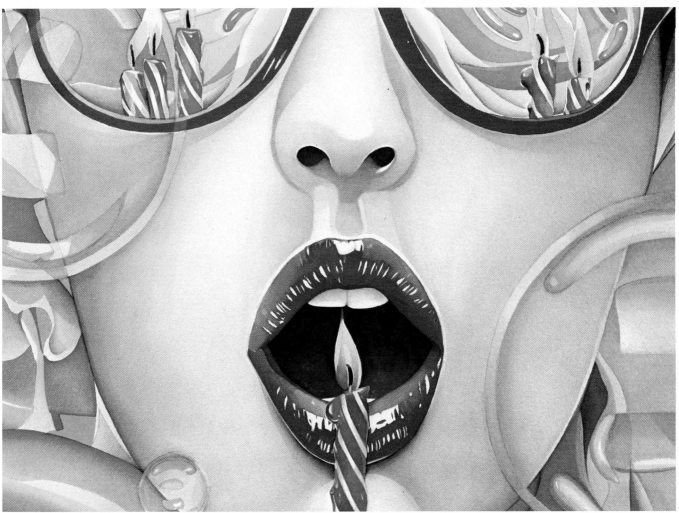

138
Artist: **JANET MAGER**
Art Director: Gill Fishman
Client: Rainboworld
Category: Institutional

139
Artist: **STEVEN H. STROUD**
Art Director: Jack Tauss
Publisher: The Franklin Library
Category: Book

140
Artist: **KENNETH FRANCIS DEWEY**
Art Director: Jack Tauss
Publisher: The Franklin Library
Category: Book

141
Artist: **JACK UNRUH**
Art Director: Steve Miller
Client: Triton Oil & Gas
Category: Institutional

142
Artist: **CHARLES TAZE DE MUTH**
Category: Institutional

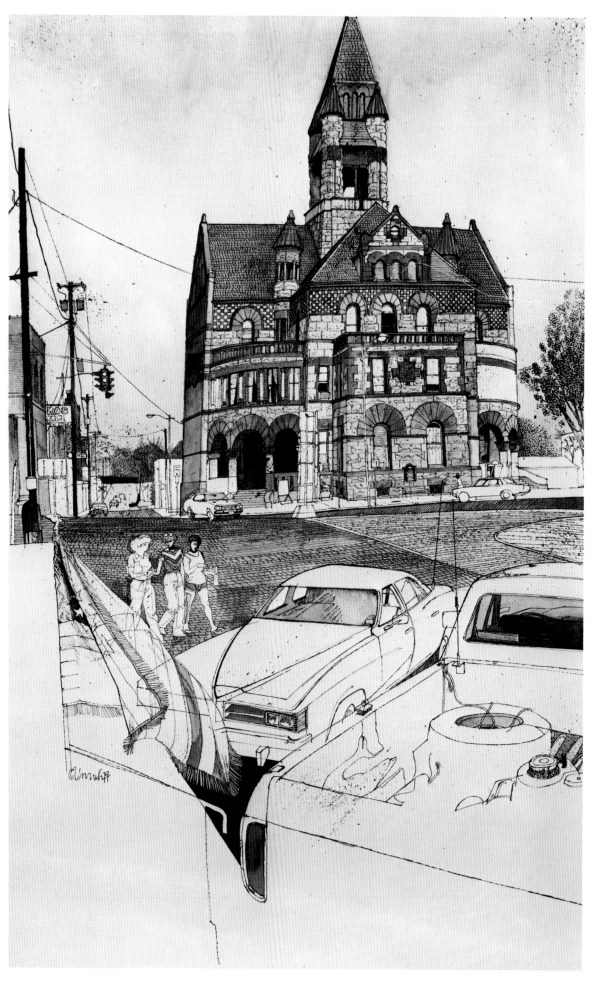

143
Artist: **JACK UNRUH**
Art Director: Steve Miller
Client: Triton Oil & Gas
Category: Institutional

144
Artist: **HARRY A. DEVLIN**
Art Director: Jeffrey A. Devlin
Category: Institutional
Special Past Chairmen's Committee Award

145
Artist: **GERRY CONTRERAS**
Category: Advertising

146
Artist: **FRED OTNES**
Art Director: Jack Tauss
Publisher: The Franklin Library
Category: Book

147
Artist: **MITCHELL HOOKS**
Art Director: Jack Tauss
Publisher: The Franklin Library
Category: Book

149
Artist: **JERRY PINKNEY**
Art Director: Jack Tauss
Publisher: The Franklin Library
Category: Book

148
Artist: **BILL CHARMATZ**
Art Director: Tamara Schneider
Magazine: Seventeen
Category: Editorial

150
Artist: **JON McINTOSH**
Art Director: Katy Aldrich
Publication: Boston Globe
Category: Editorial

151
Artist: **DAVID MACAULAY**
Art Director: Walter Lorraine
Publisher: Houghton Mifflin
Category: Book

152
Artist: **DAVID MACAULAY**
Art Director: Walter Lorraine
Publisher: Houghton Mifflin
Category: Book

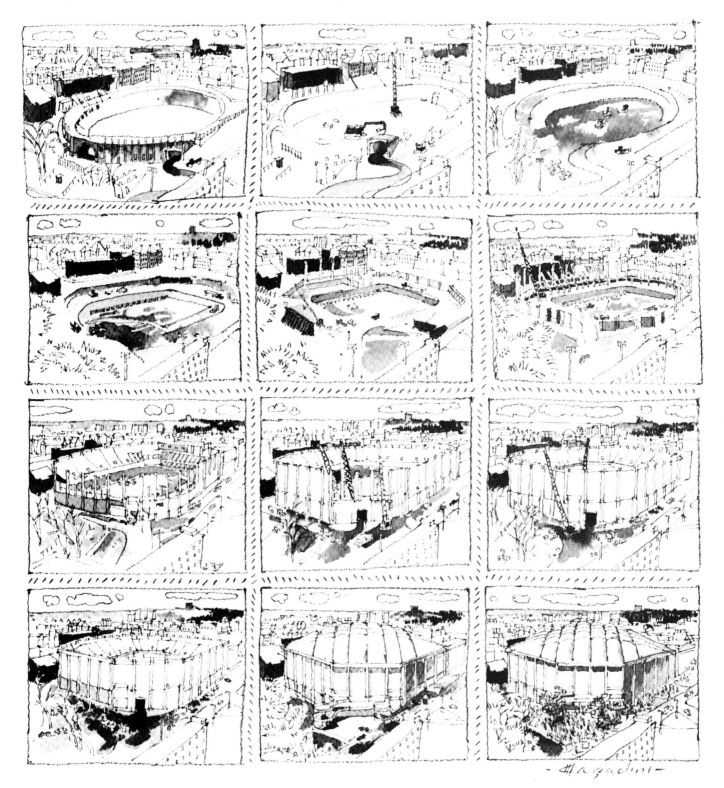

153
Artist: **CHRISTOPHER MAGADINI**
Art Director: David May
Client: Syracuse University
Category: Institutional

National Geographic photographer

Colorful 'SPARKY' SMITH, 67, served as King in 1977... re-elected in 1980.

Elected to her first term as Hobo Queen, 'CINDERBOX' CINDY is a 28-year-old rubber hobo (hitchhiker) from Texas...

'Frying Pan Jack' has been on the road for 56 years. He set up the kitchen at the hobo jungle

Former King 'Slow-Motion Shorty' is back for the first time in 4 years. Heart problems have put a damper on his rail-riding.

154
Artist: **GARY KELLEY**
Art Director: Denis Hagen
Agency: Bozell-Jacobs
Client: Northern Natural Gas
Category: Editorial

155
Artist: **GEORGE JONES**
Art Director: Soren Noring
Publisher: Reader's Digest
Category: Book

156
Artist: **TOM BLOOM**
Category: Institutional

157
Artist: **TOM BLOOM**
Category: Institutional

158
Artist: **BRALDT BRALDS**
Art Director: Bob Defrin
Client: Scotti Brothers Records
Category: Advertising

159
Artist: **MARK HESS**
Art Director: Lidia Ferrara
Publisher: Alfred A. Knopf, Inc.
Category: Book

160
Artist: **ALBERT KRAMER**
Art Director: Dennis Tani
Agency: Robert Runyan & Associates
Client: Varian Associates
Category: Institutional

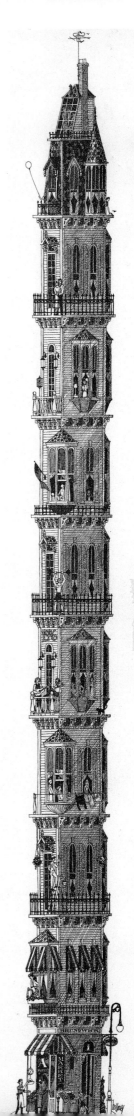

161
Artist: **SEYMOUR CHWAST**
Art Director: Edward A. Hamilton
Client: Art Institute of Fort Lauderdale
Category: Institutional

162
Artist: **BOB HOLLOWAY**
Category: Institutional

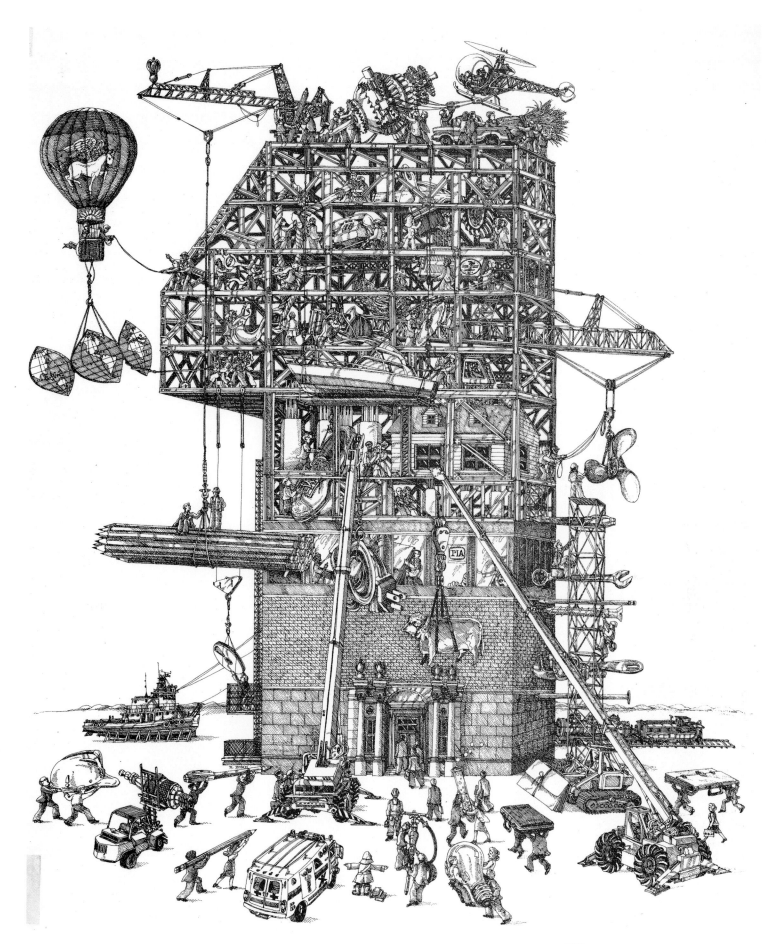

163
Artist: **ROBERT JOHN BYRD**
Art Directors: Jack Byrne/Lou Ford
Client: Insurance Co. of North America
Category: Institutional

164
Artist: **BOB CROFUT**
Category: Book

165
Artist: **BOB CROFUT**
Category: Editorial

166
Artist: **MILTON GLASER**
Art Director: Milton Glaser
Client: The Friends of Vista
Category: Advertising

167
Artist: **MILTON GLASER**
Art director: Milton Glaser
Client: N.Y. State Department of Commerce
Category: Advertising

168
Artist: **JAMES McMULLAN**
Art Director: Edward A. Hamilton
Client: Art Institute of Pittsburgh
Category: Institutional
Gold Medal

JAMES McMULLAN RETROSPECTIVE·NOVEMBER 29TH-DECEMBER 19TH

YOU ARE CORDIALLY INVITED TO THE OPENING ON THURSDAY, NOVEMBER 29TH, FROM 5:30-7:30 PM, THE VISUAL ARTS MUSEUM, 209 EAST 23RD STREET, NEW YORK CITY 10010. MONDAY THROUGH THURSDAY, NOON TO 9:00 PM, FRIDAY, 11:00 AM TO 4:30 PM. CLOSED WEEKENDS.

169
Artist: **JAMES McMULLAN**
Art Directors: Richard A. Wilde/Ayelet Bender
Client: School of Visual Arts
Category: Institutional

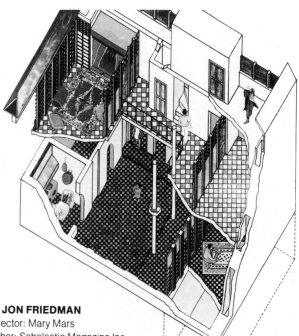

170
Artist: **JON FRIEDMAN**
Art Director: Mary Mars
Publisher: Scholastic Magazine Inc.
Category: Book

171
Artist: **JOHN BUXTON**
Art Director: Larry Taylor
Client: Aluminum Co. of America
Category: Institutional

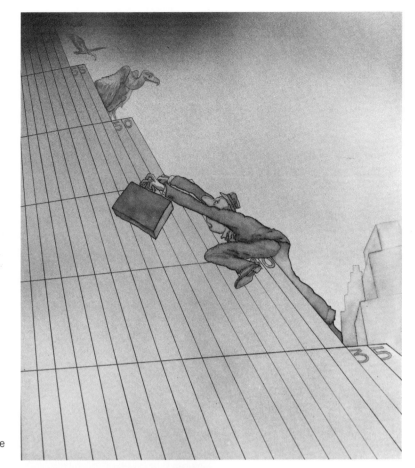

172
Aritst: **MICHAEL FOREMAN**
Art Director: Stan Corfman
Client: Marathon World Magazine
Category: Institutional

173
Artist: **LOUIS FECK**
Art Director: Len Leone
Publisher: Bantam Books
Category: Book

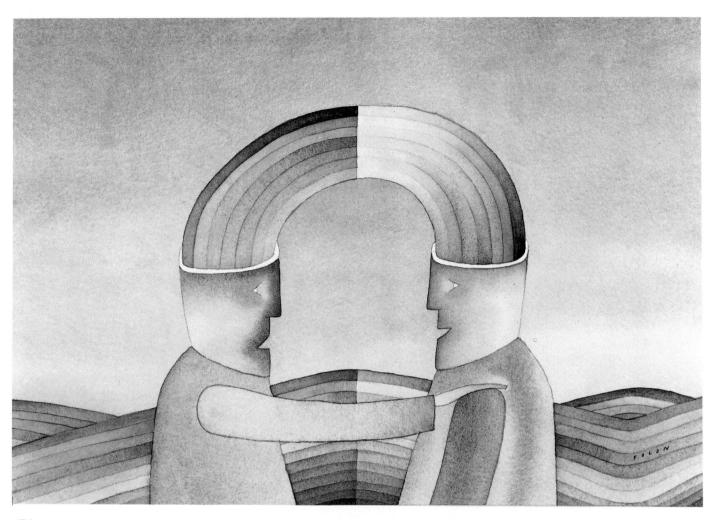

174
Artist: **FOLON**
Art Directors: Tom Staebler/T. Kouvatsos
Magazine: Playboy
Category: Editorial

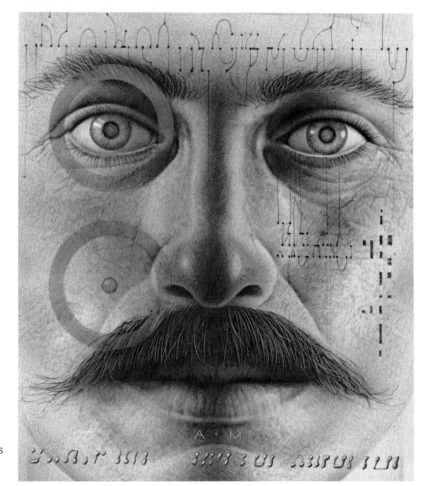

175
Artist: **ALAN MAGEE**
Art Director: Milton Charles
Publisher: Pocket Books
Category: Book

176
Artist: **JEMERSON**
Client: Indiana Credit Union League
Category: Institutional

177
Artist: **DAGMAR FRINTA**
Category: Institutional

178
Artist: **DAGMAR FRINTA**
Category: Institutional

179
Artist: **BRAD HOLLAND**
Art Director: Hans Teensma
Magazine: Rocky Mountain
Category: Editorial

180
Artist: **BRAD HOLLAND**
Art Director: Greg Paul
Publication: The Cleveland Plain Dealer Magazine
Category: Editorial

181
Artist: **MICHAEL DAVID BROWN**
Art Director: Jessie Nichols
Client: Food & Drug Administration
Category: Editorial

182
Artist: **MICHAEL DAVID BROWN**
Art Director: Jessie Nichols
Client: Food & Drug Administration
Category: Editorial

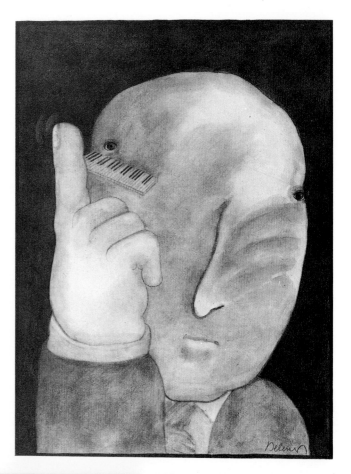

183
Artist: **ETIENNE DELESSERT**
Art Director: Etienne Delessert
Client: Gala de l'Union
Category: Editorial

184
Artist: **DAVID PLOURDE**
Art Director: Jim McFarland
Agency: Sudler & Hennessey
Client: Parke-Davis
Category: Advertising

185
Artist: **ALAN MAGEE**
Art Director: Milton Charles
Publisher: Pocket Books
Category: Book

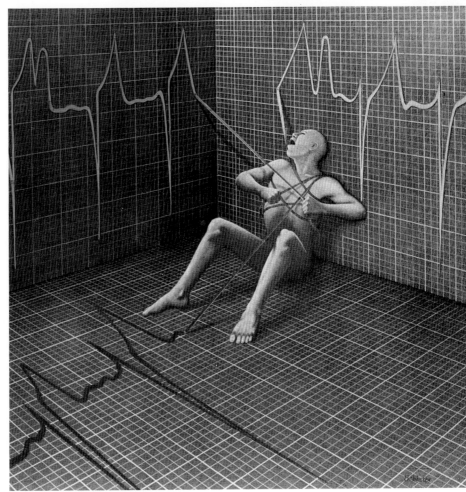

186
Artist: **BRUCE SCHLUTER**
Art Director: Jane Cullen
Client: Ciba-Geigy
Category: Institutional

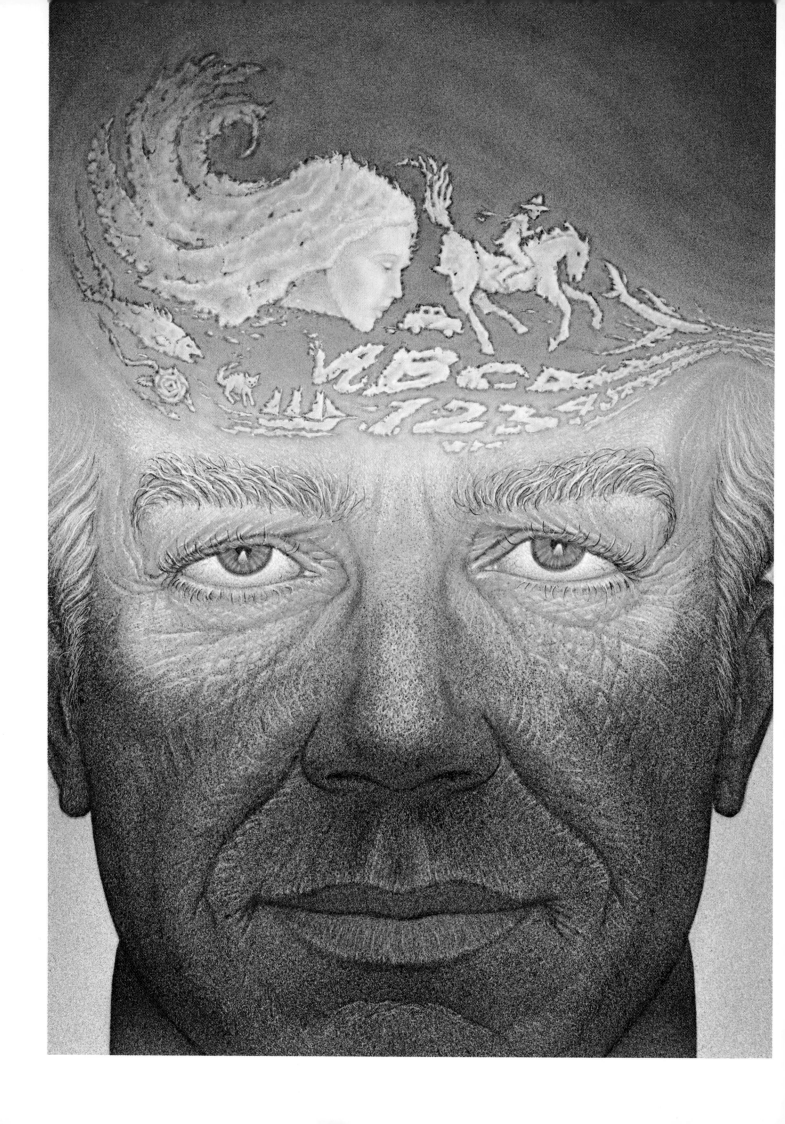

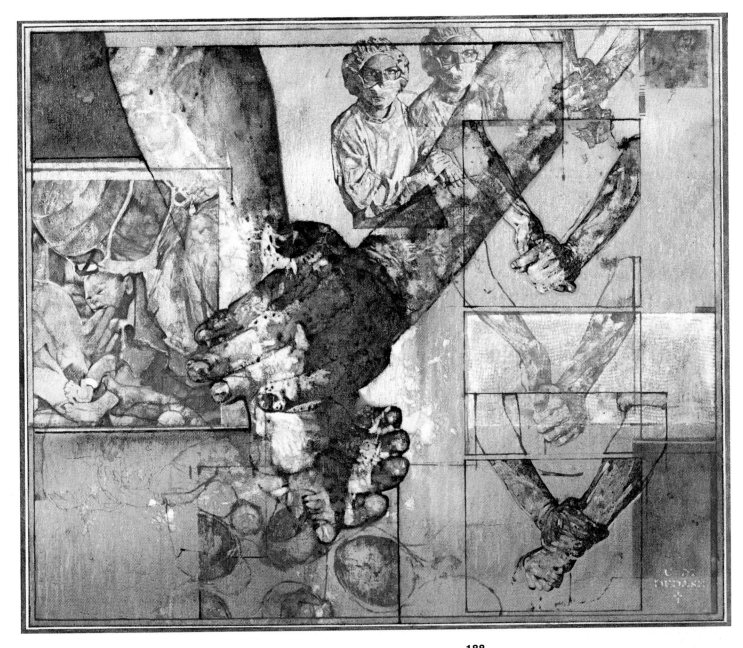

188
Artist: **MICHAEL DUDASH**
Art Director: Bob Durling
Agency: Ruvane-Leverte
Client: Surgikos, Inc.
Category: Editorial

187
Artist: **ED SOYKA**
Art Directors: Mary Zisk/Frank Rothmann
Magazine: Science Digest
Category: Editorial

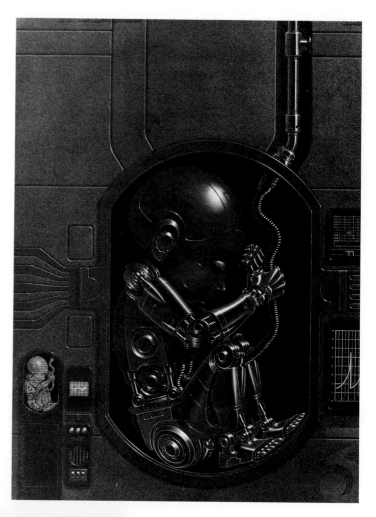

189
Artist: **THOMAS WARKENTIN**
Art Director: John Workman
Magazine: Heavy Metal
Category: Editorial

190
Artist: **De Es SCHWERTBERGER**
Art Director: Bob Heimall
Client: Cotillion Records
Category: Advertising

191
Artist: **MICHAEL BERENSTAIN**
Art Director: Cathy L. Goldsmith
Publisher: Random House
Category: Book

192
Artist: **LUCINDA COWELL**
Art Director: Jack Ribik
Publisher: Dial Press
Category: Book

193
Artist: GEOFFREY MOSS
Art Director: Larry Stires
Client: Ciba-Geigy
Category: Advertising

194
Artist: **THEO RUDNAK**
Category: Institutional

195
Artist: **GEOFFREY MOSS**
Art Director: Tina Adamek
Magazine: Post Graduate Medicine
Category: Editorial

196
Artist: **PHILIPPE WEISBECKER**
Art Director: Carveth Kramer
Magazine: Psychology Today
Category: Editorial

197
Artist: **KRIS BOYD**
Category: Institutional

198
Artist: **DON KAHN**
Art Director: Tom Lennon
Magazine: Journal of Cardiovascular Medicine
Category: Editorial

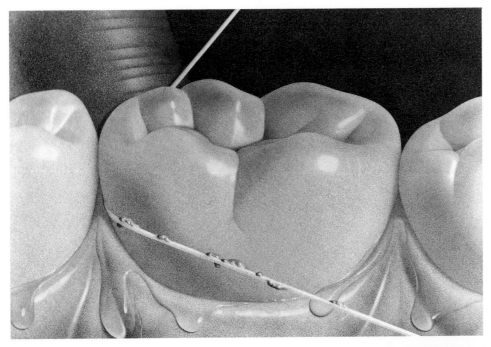

199
Artist: **EDWARD GAZZI**
Art Director: Charles Schmalz
Agency: William Douglas McAdams
Client: Johnson & Johnson
Category: Advertising

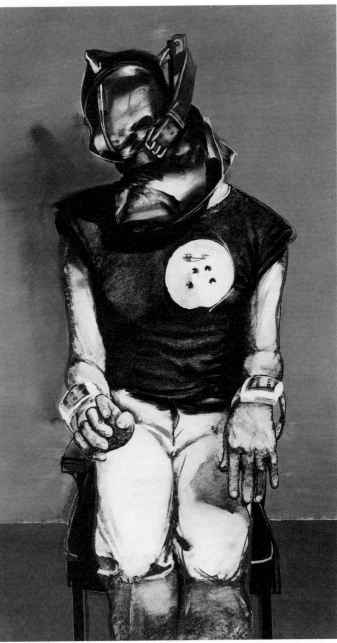

200
Artist: **MARSHALL ARISMAN**
Art Directors: Tom Staebler/Len Willis
Magazine: Playboy
Category: Editorial

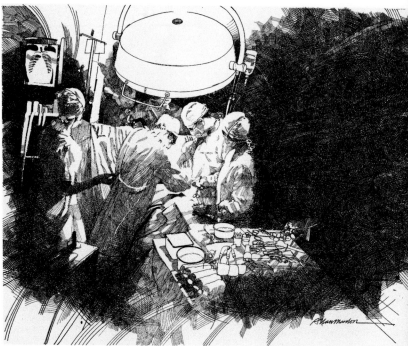

201
Artist: **ALLAN MARDON**
Art Director: Tom Von Der Linn
Publisher: Reader's Digest
Category: Book

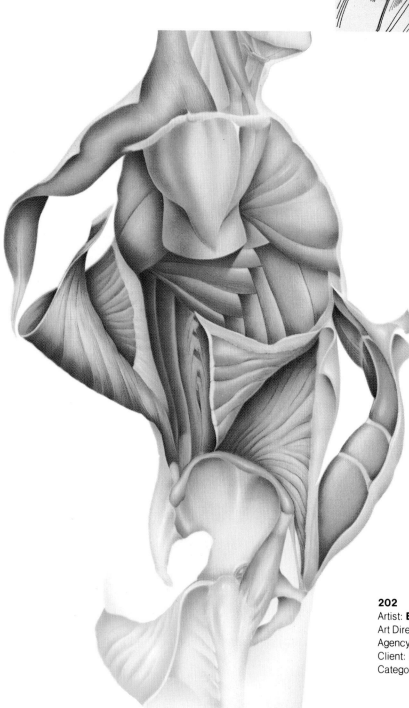

202
Artist: **ELLEN JACOBS**
Art Directors: Tom Domanico/John Trentalange
Agency: William Douglas McAdams
Client: Roche Laboratories
Category: Advertising

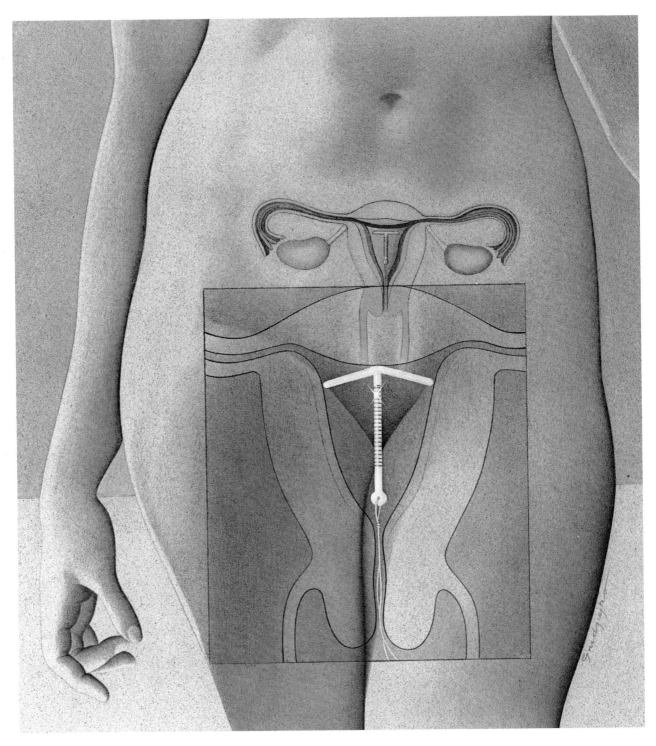

203
Artist: **ALEX GNIDZIEJKO**
Art Director: Leslie Sisman
Agency: J. Walter Thompson
Client: Searle Laboratories
Category: Advertising

204
Artist: **BRALDT BRALDS**
Art Director: Marc Eisenoff
Client: Ciba-Geigy
Category: Advertising

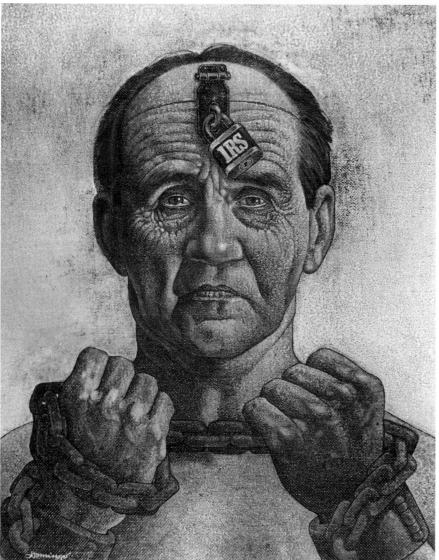

205
Artist: **RAY DOMINGO**
Art Director: Nick Dankovich
Publication: The Cleveland Plain Dealer Magazine
Category: Editorial

206
Artist: **DAVID WILCOX**
Art Director: Paula Scher
Client: CBS Records
Category: Advertising

207
Artist: **KAREN FARYNIAK**
Category: Institutional

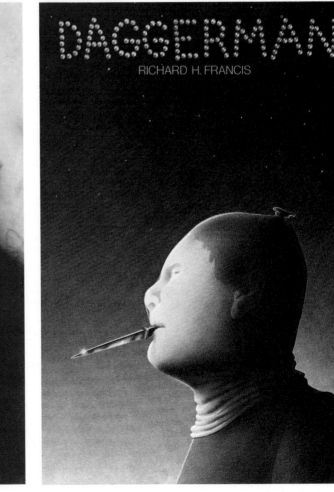

208
Artist: **FRED MARCELLINO**
Art Director: Louise Fili
Publisher: Pantheon Books
Category: Book

209
Artist: **JACK PARDUE**
Art Director: Jesse R. Nichols
Magazine: FDA Consumer
Category: Editorial

goi-ter (goi′tər), n. *Pathol.* Also, goi′tre. [t. F: (
throat]. Enlargement of the thyroid g
the rate of body metabolism. In ad
is evidenced by the formation of h
on the front and sides of the neck,
compression of the windpipe and ev

210
Artist: **RICK McCOLLUM**
Art Director: Tom Von Der Linn
Publisher: Reader's Digest
Category: Book

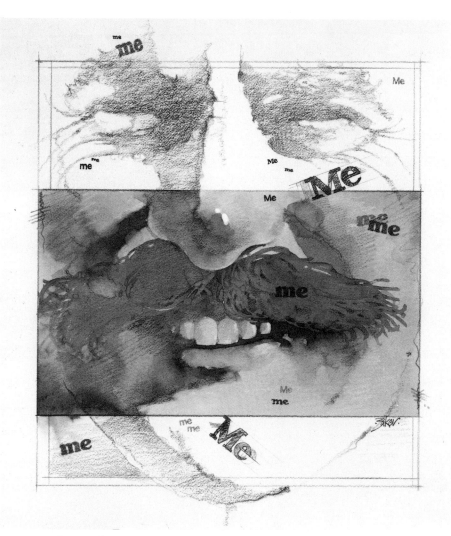

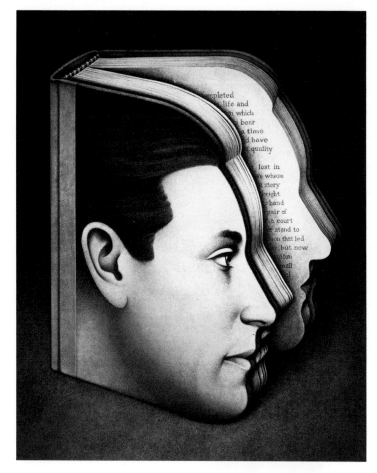

211
Artist: **SCOTT BAKER**
Art Director: Barbara Koster
Magazine: Northwest Orient Airlines ''Passages''
Category: Editorial

212
Artist: **DAVID WILCOX**
Art Director: Len Sirowitz
Agency: Rosenfeld, Sirowitz & Lawson
Client: Champion Papers
Category: Advertising

213
Artist: **ALAN E. COBER**
Art Director: Jack Tauss
Publisher: The Franklin Library
Category: Book

214
Artist: **ALAN E. COBER**
Art Director: Jack Tauss
Publisher: The Franklin Library
Category: Book

215
Artist: **ALAN E. COBER**
Art Director: Jack Tauss
Publisher: The Franklin Library
Category: Book

216
Artist: **WILSON McLEAN**
Art Director: Len Sirowitz
Agency: Rosenfeld, Sirowitz & Lawson
Client: Champion International Corp.
Category: Advertising

217
Artist: **PETER FIORE**
Art Director: Tina Adamek
Magazine: Post Graduate Medicine
Category: Editorial

218
Artist: **STEVE DE SHETLER**
Category: Editorial

219
Artist: **LISA YOUNG**
Category: Advertising

220
Artist: **SUE COE**
Art Directors: Michael Brock/James Kiehle
Magazine: Oui
Category: Editorial

221
Artist: **RICHARD NEWTON**
Art Director: Donald Munson
Publisher: Ballantine Books
Category: Book

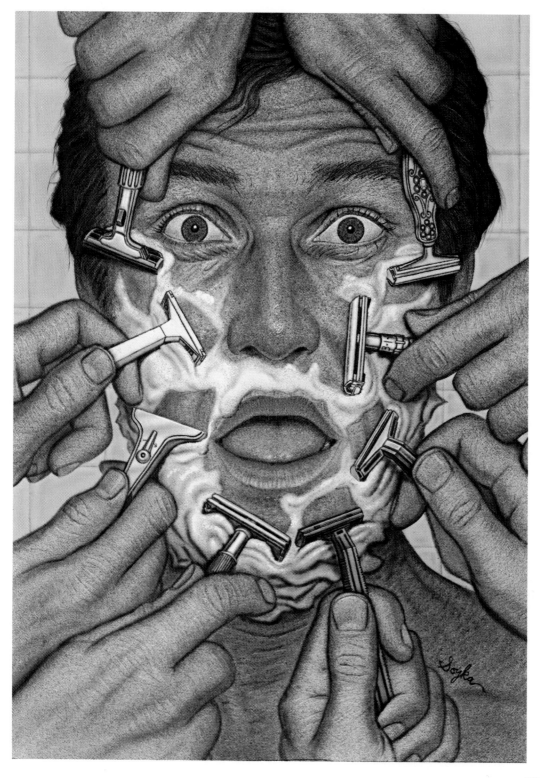

222
Artist: **ED SOYKA**
Art Director: Robert Priest
Magazine: Esquire
Category: Editorial

223
Artist: **BARRON STOREY**
Art Director: Lynn Hollyn
Publisher: Perigee Books
Category: Book

224
Artist: **DENNIS LUZAK**
Art Director: Roger Musich
Agency: William Douglas McAdams
Client: Roche Laboratories
Category: Advertising

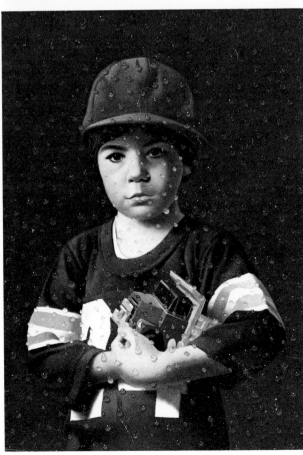

225
Artist: **R.J. SHAY**
Category: Institutional

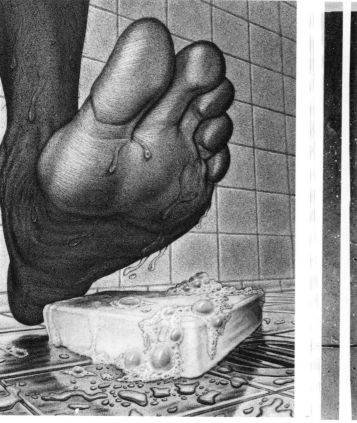

226
Artist: **ED SOYKA**
Art Director: Robert Eichinger
Client: AT&T Long Lines
Category: Advertising

227
Artist: **WAYNE DOUGLAS BARLOWE**
Category: Advertising

228
Artist: **KRIS BOYD**
Category: Institutional

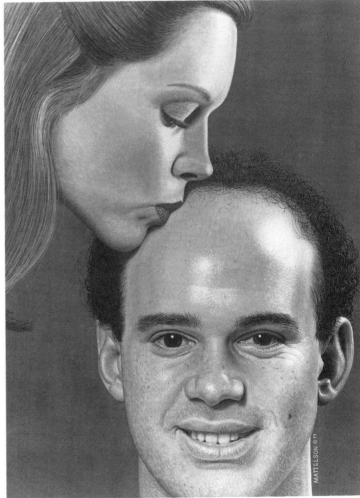

229
Artist: **MARVIN MATTELSON**
Art Director: Michael Brock
Magazine: Oui
Category: Editorial

230
Artist: **SUSAN STILLMAN**
Art Director: Jim Horne
Client: Sandoz Pharmaceuticals
Category: Institutional

231
Artist: **ROBERT HEINDEL**
Art Director: John deCesare
Client: Roche Laboratories
Category: Institutional

232
Artist: **MITCHELL HOOKS**
Art Director: Marion Davis
Publisher: Reader's Digest
Category: Book

233
Artist: **NORM WALKER**
Art Director: Donald E. Munson
Publisher: Ballantine Books
Category: Book

234
Artist: **GARY KELLEY**
Client: Hellman Design Associates
Category: Book

235
Artist: **CHARLES SANTORE**
Art Director: Elmer Pizzi
Agency: Gray & Rogers
Client: Diamond Shamrock
Category: Advertising

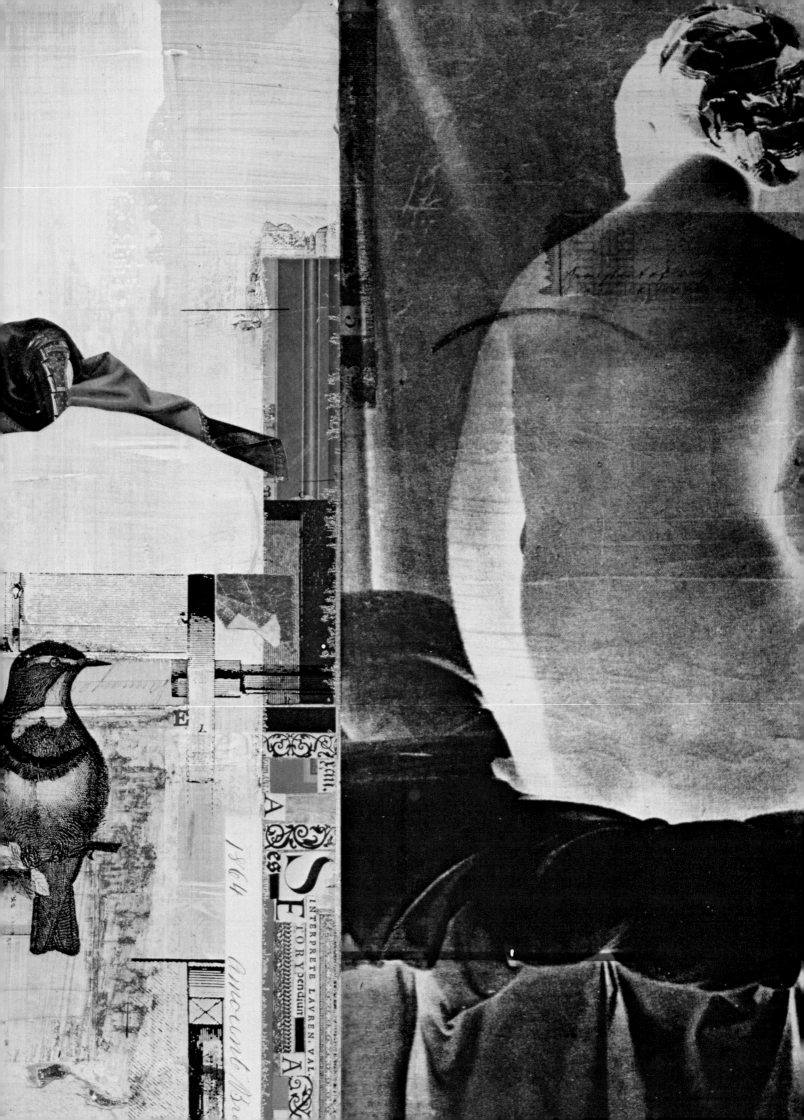

237
Artist: **FRED OTNES**
Client: Artists Associates
Category: Advertising

236
Artist: **FRED OTNES**
Art Director: John deCesare
Client: Art Directors Association of Iowa
Category: Institutional

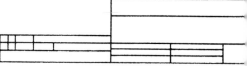

238
Artist: **MURRAY TINKELMAN**
Art Director: Herb Lubalin
Publication: U & l.c.
Category: Institutional

239
Artist: **MURRAY TINKELMAN**
Art Director: Herb Lubalin
Publication: U & l.c.
Category: Institutional

240
Artist: **MURRAY TINKELMAN**
Art Director: Herb Lubalin
Publication: U & l.c.
Category: Institutional

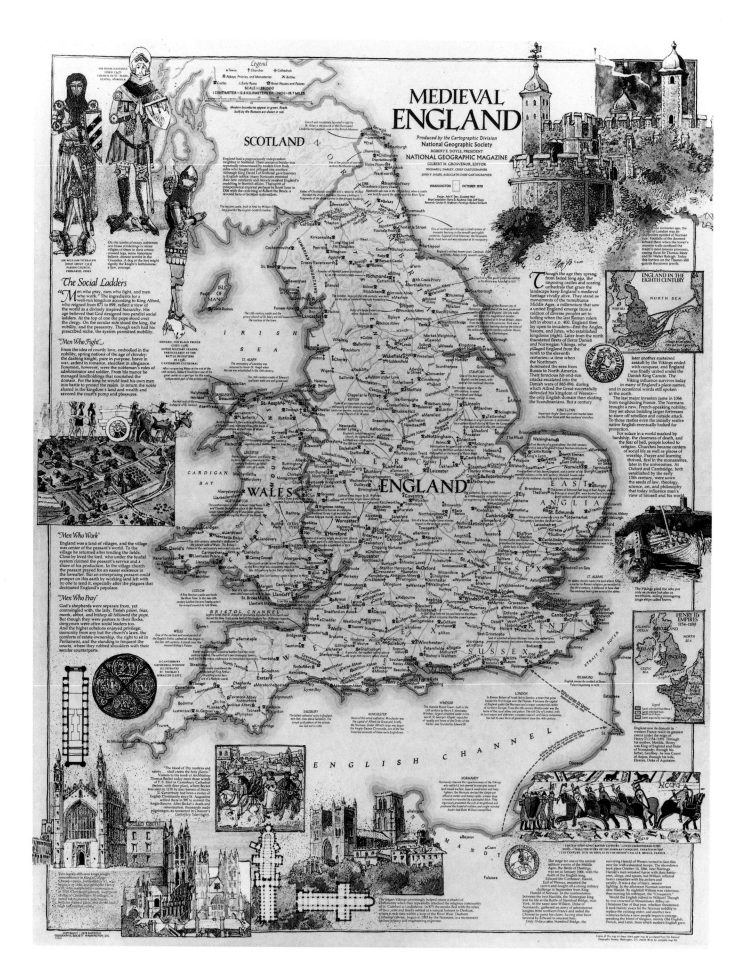

MEDIEVAL ENGLAND

Produced by the Cartographic Division
National Geographic Society
ROBERT E. DOYLE, PRESIDENT
NATIONAL GEOGRAPHIC MAGAZINE
GILBERT M. GROSVENOR, EDITOR

RICHARD J. DARLEY, CHIEF CARTOGRAPHER
JOHN F. SHUPE, ASSOCIATE CHIEF CARTOGRAPHER

WASHINGTON OCTOBER 1979

Artist: **DICK SCHLECHT**
Art Director: Jack Dorr
Magazine: National Geographic
Category: Editorial

242
Artist: **FRED OTNES**
Art Director: Nelson Pollack
Client: Gilbert Color Systems
Category: Advertising

243
Artist: **NORMAN GREEN**
Art Directors: Emil Micha/Andrew Kner
Publisher: Bantam Books
Category: Book

244
Artists: **RICHARD COHEN/JON TOWNLEY**
Art Director: Frank Devino
Magazine: Omni
Category: Editorial

245
Artist: **CHRIS SPOLLEN**
Art Director: Joseph Connolly
Magazine: Boy's Life
Category: Editorial

246
Artist: **TERRANCE LINDALL**
Art Director: John Workman
Client: Heavy Metal
Category: Institutional

247
Artist: **LEN SIROWITZ**
Art Director: Len Sirowitz
Agency: Rosenfeld, Sirowitz & Lawson
Client: Champion International Corp.
Category: Advertising

248
Artist: **GREGORY MANCHESS**
Art Director: Jeff Dorman
Magazine: Omni
Category: Editorial

249
Artist: **CAROL WALD**
Art Director: Lester Barnett
Client: Ciba-Geigy
Category: Advertising

250
Artist: **CHRIS VAN ALLSBURG**
Art Director: Walter Lorraine
Publisher: Houghton Mifflin Co.
Category: Book

251
Artist: **NITA ENGLE**
Art Director: Marion Davis
Publisher: Reader's Digest
Category: Book

252
Artist: **NITA ENGLE**
Art Directors: Don Duffy/Don Hedin
Magazine: Reader's Digest
Category: Editorial

253
Artist: **HOWARD KOSLOW**
Category: Editorial

254
Artist: **JAIME QUINTERO**
Art Director: Rodney Williams
Magazine: Science 80
Category: Editorial

255
Artist: **ALEX GNIDZIEJKO**
Art Director: Modesto Torre
Magazine: McCall's
Category: Editorial

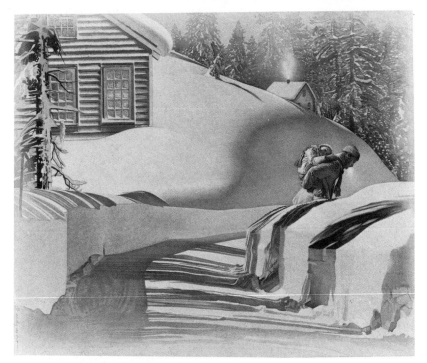

256
Artist: **ALEX GNIDZIEJKO**
Art Director: Modesto Torre
Magazine: McCall's
Category: Editorial

257
Artist: **BARRY ROSS**
Art Director: Daryl Herrmann
Magazine: Golf
Category: Editorial

258
Artist: **BOB McGINNIS**
Art Director: Len Leone
Publisher: Bantam Books
Category: Book

259
Artist: **RICHARD SPARKS**
Art Director: Lynn Hollyn
Publisher: Coward, McCann & Geoghegan
Category: Book

260
Artist: **CHRISTOPHER FOSS**
Art Director: David M. Seager
Publisher: National Geographic Society
Category: Book

261
Artist: **CHRISTOPHER FOSS**
Art Director: David M. Seager
Publisher: National Geographic Society
Category: Book

262
Artist: **JOHN THOMPSON**
Art Director: Jack Tauss
Publisher: The Franklin Library
Category: Book

263
Artist: **JOHN THOMPSON**
Art Director: Marion Davis
Publisher: Reader's Digest
Category: Book

264
Artist: **BILL JAMES**
Category: Institutional

265
Artist: **BILL JAMES**
Category: Institutional

266
Artist: **LAURA CORNELL**
Art Director: Don Dame
Client: Windemere Press
Category: Institutional

267
Artist: **LAURA CORNELL**
Art Director: Don Dame
Client: Windemere Press
Category: Institutional

268
Artist: **LAURA CORNELL**
Art Director: Don Dame
Client: Windemere Press
Category: Institutional

269
Artist: **MARGARET CUSACK**
Art Director: Hal Goluboff
Agency: Mathieu, Gerfen & Bresner
Client: Great Waters of France
Category: Advertising

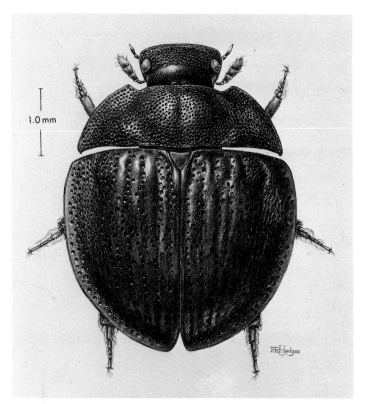

270
Artist: **ROBERT JOHN BYRD**
Art Director: Elmer Pizzi
Agency: Gray & Rogers
Client: Grit
Category: Advertising

271
Artist: **ELAINE R. HODGES**
Client: Smithsonian Institution
Category: Institutional

272
Artist: **DON IVAN PUNCHATZ**
Art Director: Gene Light
Publisher: Warner Books
Category: Book

273
Artist: **JACK UNRUH**
Art Directors: Jim Darilek/Sybil Broyles
Magazine: Texas Monthly
Category: Editorial

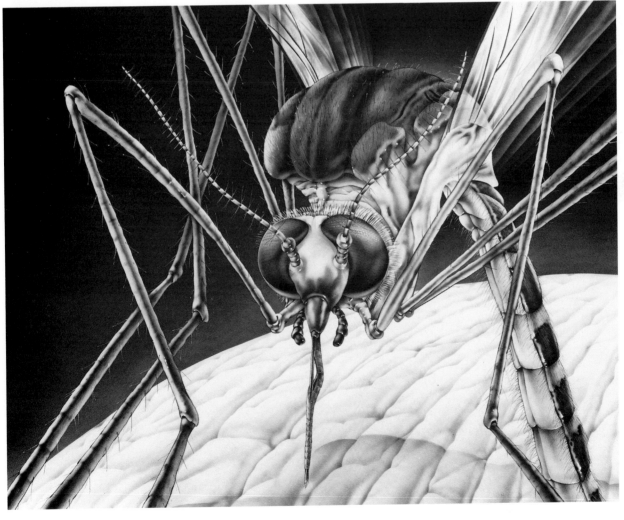

274
Artist: **MICHAEL DEAN**
Art Director: Peggy McDaniel
Magazine: Houston City
Category: Editorial

275
Artist: **RICHARD HULL**
Art Director: Lee Shaw
Magazine: The New Era
Category: Editorial

276
Artist: **TERRY WICKART**
Category: Editorial

277
Artist: **MARION NEEDHAM KRUPP**
Category: Advertising

278
Artist: **ROBERT HYNES**
Art Director: Howard Paine
Magazine: National Geographic
Category: Editorial

279
Artist: **BRALDT BRALDS**
Art Director: Maxine Davidowitz
Magazine: Redbook
Category: Editorial

280
Artist: **ROB WOOD**
Agency: Stansbury, Ronsaville Wood Inc.
Client: Cascio-Wolf, Inc.
Category: Institutional

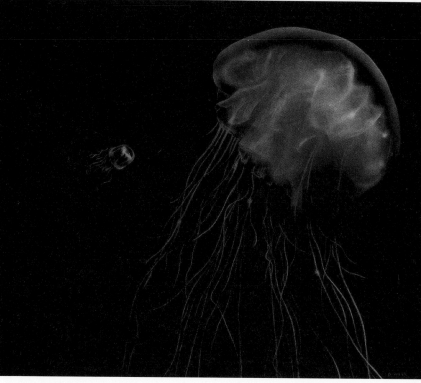

281
Artist: **ROB WOOD**
Agency: Stansbury, Ronsaville Wood Inc.
Client: Cascio-Wolf Inc.
Category: Institutional

282
Artist: **ARTHUR SHILSTONE**
Art Director: Victor J. Closi
Magazine: Field & Stream
Category: Editorial

283
Artist: **JAMES GRIFFIN**
Art Director: Barbara G. Hennessy
Publisher: Viking Penguin Inc.
Category: Book

284
Artist: **SIMMS TABACK**
Art Director: Carol Carson
Magazine: Scholastic
Category: Editorial

285
Artist: **RONALD SNYDER**
Category: Book

287
Artist: **JUDY CLIFFORD**
Art Director: Meredith Carpentier
Publisher: Frederick Warne & Co. Inc.
Category: Book

286
Artist: **ARVIS STEWART**
Art Director: Zelda Haber
Publisher: Macmillian Publishing Co.
Category: Book

288
Artist: **CRAIG C. CALSBEEK**
Art Director: Diana Marie Kaylan
Client: Boatz
Category: Advertising

289
Artist: **GEORGE FOUNDS**
Art Directors: Lynda Barber/Cynthia Basil
Publisher: Morrow Junior Books
Category: Book

290
Artist: **DAVID NOYES**
Category: Book

291
Artist: **PAUL GIOVANOPOULOS**
Category: Institutional

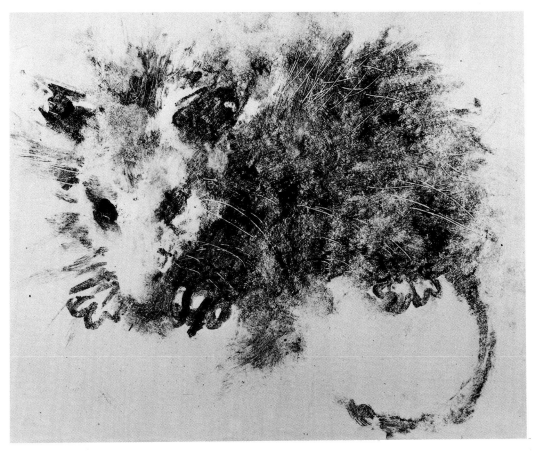

292
Artist: **KENNETH KRAFCHEK**
Category: Institutional

293
Artist: **ROBERT J. LEE**
Art Directors: John Witt/Cathy de Martin
Agency: Ruvane Leverte
Client: Astra Pharmaceuticals
Category: Institutional

294
Artist: **BOB ZIERING**
Client: Jerry Anton
Category: Institutional

295
Artist: **ROBERT LO GRIPPO**
Art Director: Edward Rofheart
Publisher: Popular Library
Category: Institutional

296
Artist: **MICHAEL HAGUE**
Art Director: Jeffrey Willsey
Client: Sunrise Publications Inc.
Category: Institutional

297
Artist: **WALTER FRANK BOMAR**
Client: U.S. Government
Category: Institutional

298
Artist: **GARY KELLEY**
Art Director: Mick Ascherl
Client: Mutual of Omaha
Category: Advertising

299
Artist: **TOM McKEVENY**
Art Director: Judy Lee
Publisher: Simon & Schuster
Category: Book

300
Artist: **MICHAEL MANZ**
Art Directors: Werner Kustermann/William Gregory
Publisher: Reader's Digest
Category: Book

301
Artist: **WALT SPITZMILLER**
Art Director: Gary Gretter
Magazine: Sports Afield
Category: Editorial

302
Artist: **CHRIS DUKE**
Art Director: Char Lappan
Publisher: Little Brown & Company
Category: Book

303
Artist: **LINDA GIST**
Art Director: Jack Taylor
Agency: Gray & Rogers
Client: Caulk
Category: Advertising

304
Artist: **ROSEKRANS HOFFMAN**
Art Director: Kathleen Tucker
Publisher: Albert Whitman & Co.
Category: Book

305
Artist: **NED SEIDLER**
Art Director: Bill Palmstrom
Magazine: National Geographic
Category: Editorial

306
Artist: **DAVID M. BECK**
Agency: Higgins, Hegner, Genovese
Magazine: Playboy
Category: Editorial

307
Artist: **MARVIN MATTELSON**
Art Directors: Mike Schell / Joe Pouy
Agency: Young & Rubicam
Category: Advertising

308
Artist: **WILLIAM HARMUTH**
Art Director: Jack Tauss
Publisher: The Franklin Library
Category: Book

309
Artist: **CRAIG NELSON**
Category: Editorial

311
Artist: **HEATHER COOPER**
Art Director: Peter Nevraumont
Client: Ruby Street
Category: Institutional

310
Artist: **SUSAN JEFFERS**
Art Director: Atha Tehon
Publisher: The Dial Press
Category: Book

312
Artist: **HEATHER COOPER**
Art Director: Peter Nevraumont
Client: Ruby Street
Category: Institutional

313
Artist: **REVILO**
Art Director: Don Dame
Client: Windemere Press
Category: Institutional

314
Artist: **JOANNE SCRIBNER**
Art Director: Bruce Hall
Publisher: Dell Publishing
Category: Book

315
Artist: **CAROL GILLOT**
Category: Book

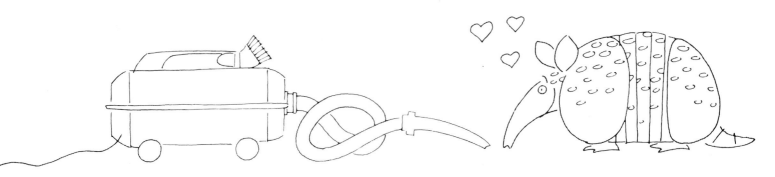

316
Artist: **BILL BREWER**
Client: Hallmark Cards
Category: Institutional

317
Artist: **RICHARD EGIELSKI**
Art Director: Michael DiCapua
Publisher: Farrar, Straus & Giroux
Category: Book

318
Artist: **PAULINE ELLISON**
Art Director: Len Leone
Publisher: Bantam Books
Category: Book

320
Artist: **ED LINDLOF**
Art Director: John Weaver
Client: Digicon, Inc.
Category: Institutional

319
Artist: **NORMAN MACDONALD**
Art Director: Brian Smith
Magazine: Aramco World
Category: Institutional

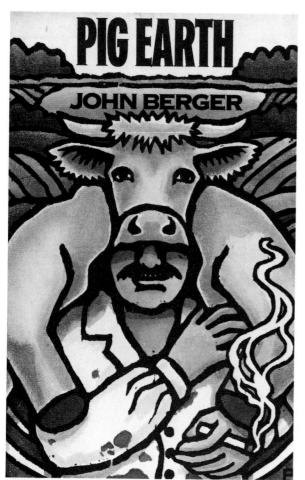

321
Artist: **BASCOVE**
Art Director: Louise Fili
Publisher: Pantheon Books
Category: Book

322
Artist: **BASCOVE**
Art Director: Krystyna Skalski
Publisher: Harcourt, Brace, Jovanovich
Category: Book

323
Artist: **WILSON McLEAN**
Art Director: Jitsuo Hoashi
Client: Japanese Bartenders Association
Category: Advertising

324
Artist: **MARK KAPLAN**
Art Director: Mike Jimenez
Publisher: Scholastic Books
Category: Book

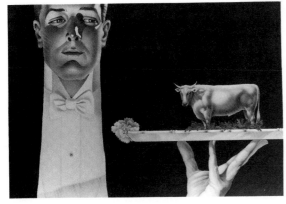

325
Artists: **DAN GLIDDEN/FLAT LIZARD**
Art Director: Jim Darilek/Sybil Broyles
Magazine: Texas Monthly
Category: Editorial

326
Artist: **TRACY BROWN**
Category: Advertising

327
Artist: **MICHAEL HAGUE**
Art Director: Janet Townsend
Publisher: Pantheon Books
Category: Book

328
Artist: **JEAN LEON HUENS**
Art Director: Bruce Hall
Publisher: Dell Publishing
Category: Book

329
Artist: **JÖZEF SUMICHRAST**
Art Director: Al Swanstrom
Agency: Campbell-Mithun
Client: Vopi Process
Category: Advertising

330
Artist: **SANDY HUFFAKER**
Category: Institutional

331
Artist: **DAGMAR FRINTA**
Art Director: Nina Scerbo
Magazine: McCall's Working Mother
Category: Editorial

332
Artist: **JAMES C. CHRISTENSEN**
Category: Book

333
Artist: **REYNOLD RUFFINS**
Client: Charles Scribner's Sons
Category: Institutional

334
Artist: **REYNOLD RUFFINS**
Publisher: Charles Scribner's Sons
Category: Institutional

335
Artist: **JOYCE ANN SCHARF**
Art Director: Elaine H. Duillo
Category: Institutional

336
Artist: **BILL PROCHNOW**
Art Director: Dugald Stermer
Magazine: Communication Arts
Category: Editorial

337
Artist: **BILL PROCHNOW**
Art Director: Dugald Stermer
Magazine: Communication Arts
Category: Editorial

338
Artist: **NORM WALKER**
Art Director: Jerry Counihan
Publisher: Ballantine Books
Category: Book

339
Artist: **JEFF KRONEN**
Category: Book

340
Artist: **FRANK MAYO**
Category: Editorial

341
Artist: **JOSEPH CIARDIELLO**
Client: Moonlight Press
Category: Institutional

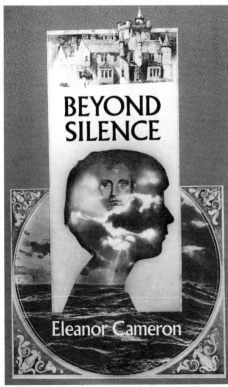

342
Artist: **MICHAEL HESLOP**
Art Director: Riki Levinson
Publisher: E.P. Dutton
Category: Book

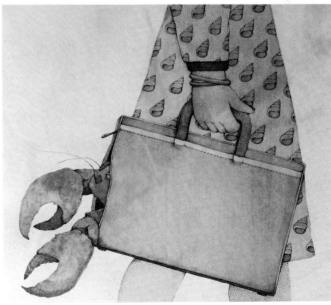

343
Artist: **DAGMAR FRINTA**
Art Director: Nina Scerbo
Magazine: McCall's Working Mother
Category: Editorial

344
Artist: **MARVIN MATTELSON**
Art Director: Sam Howard
Magazine: Scientific American
Category: Editorial

345
Artist: **DON WELLER**
Art Director: Greg Wilder
Client: Sun Graphics
Category: Institutional

346
Artist: **DON WELLER**
Art Director: Greg Wilder
Client: Sun Graphics
Category: Institutional

347
Artist: **CHUCK SLACK**
Art Director: Chuck Slack
Publication: Chicago Tribune
Category: Editorial

348
Artist: **JO SICKBERT**
Art Director: Robert Meyer
Client: Suntory International
Category: Advertising

349
Artist: **FRED MARCELLINO**
Art Director: Rudy Hoglund
Magazine: Time
Category: Editorial

350
Artist: **KRISTINA RODANAS**
Category: Book

OHIO BUCKEYE
Ohio

RED PINE
Minnesota

FLOWERING DOGWOOD
Missouri
Virginia

REDBUD
Oklahoma

SCARLET OAK
District of Columbia

PECAN
Texas

SINGLELEAF
PINYON
Nevada

PAPER BIRCH
New Hampshire

PONDEROSA
PINE
Montana

EASTERN
HEMLOCK
Pennsylvania

NORTHERN RED OAK
New Jersey

351
Artist: **SAL CATALANO**
Art Director: Ann King
Agency: Foote Cone & Belding
Client: U.S. Dept. of the Interior
Category: Institutional

352
Artist: **JACK UNRUH**
Art Directors: Jim Darilek/Sybil Broyles
Magazine: Texas Monthly
Category: Editorial

353
Artist: **SUE LLEWELLYN**
Client: Clifford Gallery
Category: Institutional

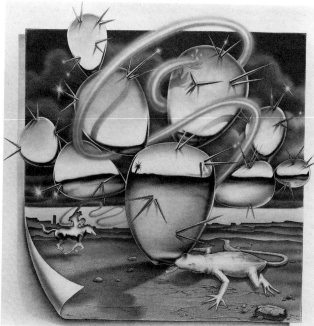

354
Artist: **MICHAEL STEIRNAGLE**
Category: Institutional

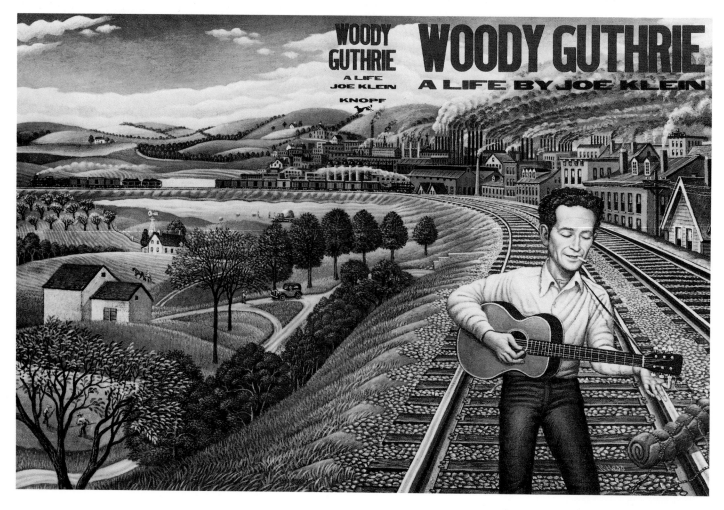

355
Artist: **RICHARD HESS**
Art Director: Lidia Ferrara
Publisher: Alfred A. Knopf, Inc.
Category: Book

356
Artist: **JÖZEF SUMICHRAST**
Art Director: Al Adas
Agency: Grant Jacoby, Inc.
Client: Sears
Category: Institutional

357
Artist: **JÖZEF SUMICHRAST**
Art Director: Marcia Wilk
Agency: Needham, Harper, Steers
Client: Anheuser-Busch
Category: Advertising

Genus: Manufacturers Hanover
Species: Correspondent Services

Loan Participator

Impac Securities Transaction Monitor

Employee Benefits Programmer

International Services

Corporate Trust Services

Transend Cash Management Services

Certificateless Depository Processor

Personal Trust Services

Investment Banking Services

359
Artist: **FRANCIS GOLDEN**
Art Director: Gary Gretter
Magazine: Sports Afield
Category: Editorial

358
Artist: **JERRY PINKNEY**
Art Director: Marty Giuricio
Agency: E.B. Wilson
Client: Manufacturers Hanover Trust
Category: Advertising

360
Artist: **DONALD D. KRAUSE**
Category: Institutional

361
Artist: **ROLAND DESCOMBES**
Category: Editorial

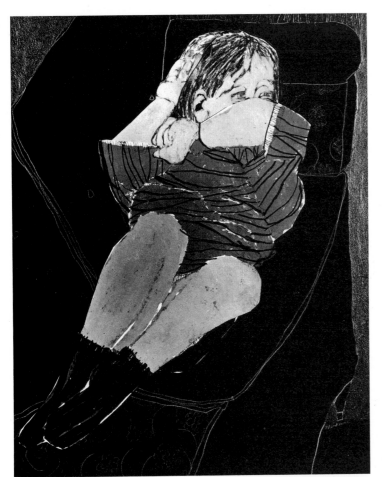

362
Artist: **JULIE SHENKMAN**
Category: Editorial

363
Artist: **ELIZABETH BENNETT**
Art Directors: Tom Staebler/Len Willis
Magazine: Playboy
Category: Editorial

364
Artist: **BOB PEAK**
Art Director: Don Smolen
Agency: Smolen, Smith, Connolly
Client: United Artists
Category: Advertising
Gold Medal

365
Artist: **RICHARD ELY**
Art Director: Barbara Schaffer
Client: Franklin Media Corp.
Category: Advertising

366
Artist: **JOAN HALL**
Art Director: Louise Fili
Publisher: Pantheon Books
Category: Book

367
Artists: **TAKI ONO/LISA POWERS**
Art Director: Michael Brock
Magazine: Oui
Category: Editorial

368
Artist: **NICHOLAS GAETANO**
Art Director: Rowan Johnson
Magazine: Penthouse
Category: Editorial

369
Artist: **MARK HESS**
Art Director: Paula Scher
Client: CBS Records
Category: Advertising

370
Artist: **ELLEN RIXFORD**
Art Director: Peter Palazzo
Magazine: Psychology Today
Category: Editorial

372
Artist: **CAROL WALD**
Category: Institutional

373
Artist: **DAVID WILCOX**
Art Director: Paula Scher
Client: CBS Records
Category: Advertising

371
Artist: **MARVIN MATTELSON**
Art Director: Carveth Kramer
Magazine: Psychology Today
Category: Editorial

374
Artist: **MARK ENGLISH**
Art Director: Robert Meyer
Client: Jack O'Grady Galleries
Category: Advertising

375
Artist: **MARA McAFEE**
Category: Book

376
Artist: **DAVID PASSALACQUA**
Art Director: Len Leone
Publisher: Bantam Books
Category: Book

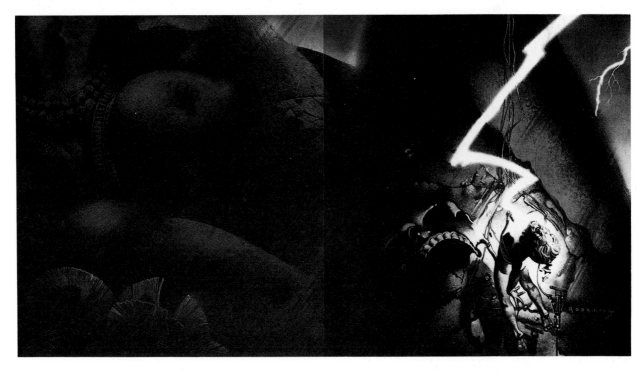

377
Artist: **ROBERT RODRIGUEZ**
Art Directors: Michael Brock/Roger Carpenter
Magazine: Oui
Category: Editorial

378
Artist: **DENNIS LUZAK**
Category: Institutional

379
Artist: **WILSON McLEAN**
Art Director: Joe Brooks
Magazine: Penthouse
Category: Editorial

380
Artist: **KEN C. HAMILTON**
Art Director: Peter Martin
Publisher: Ginn Literature
Category: Book

381
Artist: **TONY KOKINOS**
Art Director: Salvatore Lazzarotti
Magazine: Guideposts
Category: Editorial

382
Artist: **BILL JAMES**
Category: Institutional

383
Artist: **DAVID NOYES**
Category: Advertising

384
Artist: **ROBERT HEINDEL**
Art Director: John deCesare
Client: Artists Associates
Category: Institutional

385
Artist: **TONY EUBANKS**
Category: Institutional

386
Artist: **SAUL BASS**
Agency: Saul Bass/Herb Yager Assoc.
Client: The Music Center Unified Fund
Category: Advertising

387
Artist: **DAVID CHRISTIANA**
Category: Editorial

388
Artist: **MARK BOROW**
Category: Institutional

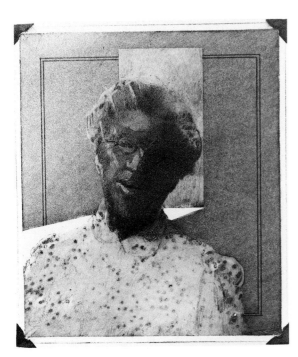

389
Artist: **REED DIXON**
Art Director: Alma Hanson
Publisher: The Economy Company
Category: Book

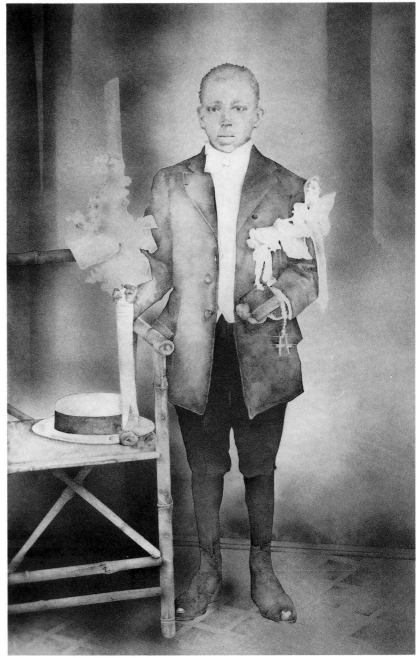

390
Artist: **SUSAN RANDSTROM**
Art Director: Robert Meyer
Client: Jack O'Grady Galleries
Category: Advertising

391
Artist: **BERNIE FUCHS**
Art Director: Anne Masters
Client: Time-Life Books Inc.
Category: Advertising

392
Artist: **JOHN BERKEY**
Category: Institutional
Special Past Chairmen's Committee Award

393
Artist: **STEVE KARCHIN**
Art Director: Dick Smith
Magazine: Communication Arts
Category: Editorial

394
Artist: **STEVE KARCHIN**
Art Director: Dick Smith
Client: RCA Records
Category: Advertising

395
Artist: **FREDERICK H. CARLSON**
Category: Advertising

396
Artist: **ALEX GNIDZIEJKO**
Art Directors: Abie Sussman/Bob Defrin
Client: Atlantic Records
Category: Advertising

397
Artist: **GARY KELLEY**
Art Director: D. Terry Williams
Client: UNI Lyric Theatre
Category: Advertising
Gold Medal

398
Artist: **ROBERT HEINDEL**
Art Director: Anne Masters
Client: Time-Life Books Inc.
Category: Advertising

399
Artist: **ROBERT HEINDEL**
Art Director: Anne Masters
Client: Time-Life Books Inc.
Category: Advertising

400
Artist: **YVONNE BUCHANAN**
Art Director: Stephanie Hill
Publication: The Village Voice
Category: Editorial

401
Artist: **JIM DENNEY**
Art Director: Jim Denney
Client: WYES-TV
Category: Advertising

402
Artist: **BOB CROFUT**
Category: Book

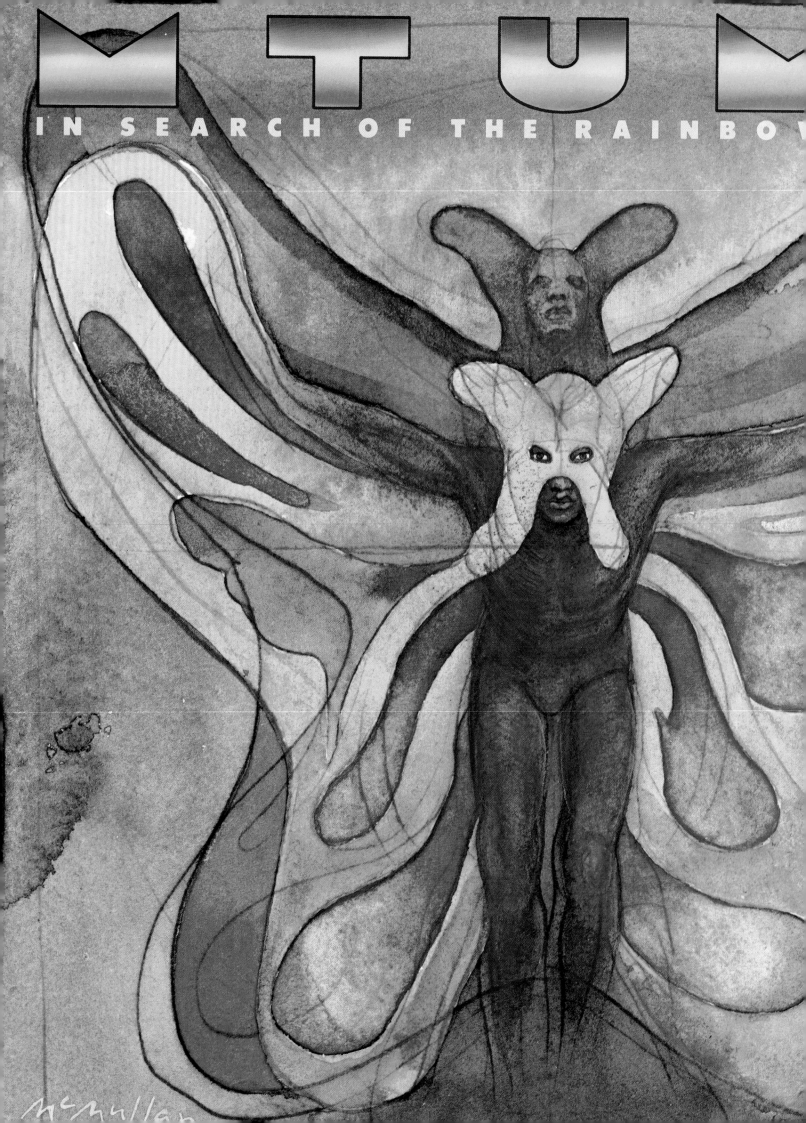

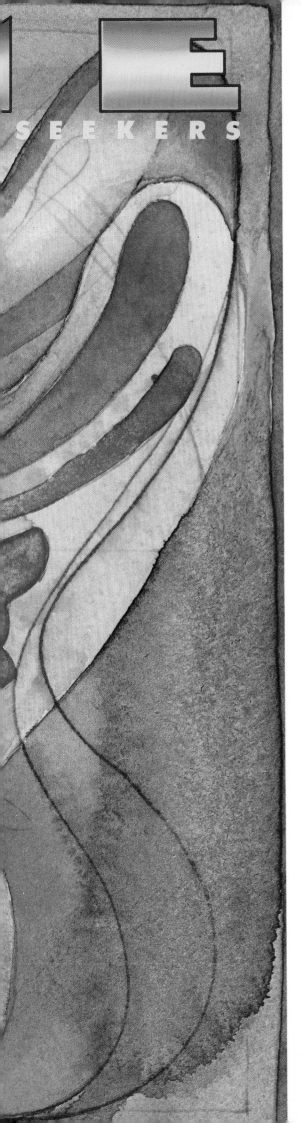

STANLEY CLARKE ROCKS, PEBBLES AND SAND

404
Artist: **ROBERT GIUSTI**
Art Director: Nancy Donald
Client: CBS Records
Category: Advertising

403
Artist: **JAMES McMULLAN**
Art Director: Paula Scher
Client: CBS Records
Category: Advertising
Award of Excellence

405
Artist: **BURT SILVERMAN**
Art Director: Susan Lyster
Agency: McCaffrey & McCall
Client: Exxon Corporation
Category: Advertising

406
Artist: **GARY KELLEY**
Art Director: Gary Kelley
Client: Waterloo-Cedar Falls Symphony
Category: Institutional

407
Artist: **R.J. SHAY**
Art Director: Al Schweitzer
Publication: St. Louis Post Dispatch
Category: Editorial

408
Artist: **BURT SILVERMAN**
Art Director: Susan Lyster
Agency: McCaffrey & McCall
Client: Exxon Corporation
Category: Advertising

409
Artist: **EDWARD SOREL**
Art Director: Henrietta Condak
Client: CBS Records
Category: Advertising

410
Artist: **BILL NELSON**
Art Director: Bill Nelson
Client: Richmond AD Club / 1980 ADDY Awards
Category: Institutional
Award of Excellence

411
Artist: **WILLIAM MANGUM**
Category: Editorial

412
Artist: **BARRON STOREY**
Art Director: Dave Seager
Client: National Geographic Records
Category: Advertising

413
Artist: **BOB PEAK**
Art Director: Anne Masters
Client: Time-Life Books Inc.
Category: Advertising

414
Artist: **RICHARD SPARKS**
Art Director: Jerry Alten
Magazine: TV Guide
Category: Editorial

415
Artist: **MICHAEL HAYNES**
Art Director: Michael Haynes
Publication: St. Louis Post Dispatch
Category: Editorial

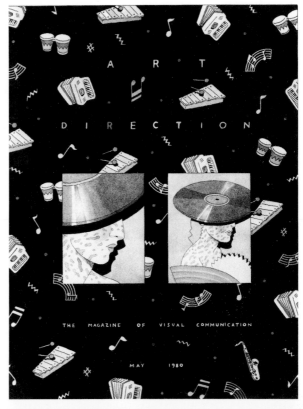

416
Artist: **STEVEN GUARNACCIA**
Art Director: Deborah Schine
Magazine: Art Direction
Category: Editorial

417
Artist: **STEPHEN RYBKA**
Category: Institutional

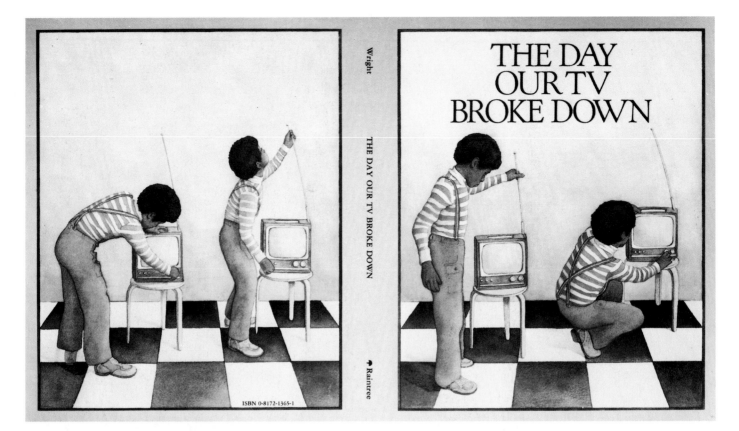

418
Artists: **BARBARA BEJNA/SHIRLEE JENSEN**
Art Director: Jane Palecek
Publisher: Raintree Publishing
Category: Book

419
Artist: **JEFF SEAVER**
Art Director: Nina Scerbo
Magazine: McCall's Working Mother
Category: Editorial

420
Artist: **MICHAEL DAVID BROWN**
Art Director: Michael David Brown
Client: Mayfair Theatre
Category: Institutional

421
Artist: **SHARON KNETTELL**
Category: Editorial

422
Artist: **JOHN JUDE PALENCAR**
Art Directors: Bernie Fuchs/Bob Heindel
Client: Lindenmeyer Paper Corp.
Category: Advertising

423
Artist: **ROBERT GIUSTI**
Art Director: Paula Scher
Client: CBS Records
Category: Advertising

424
Artist: **JOHN ALCORN**
Art Director: Henrietta Condak
Client: CBS Records
Category: Advertising

425
Artist: **JOHN BERKEY**
Art Director: Fred Grumm
Client: U.S. Navy
Category: Advertising

426
Artist: **JOHN BERKEY**
Art Director: Fred Grumm
Client: U.S. Navy
Category: Advertising

427
Artist: **JOHN BERKEY**
Art Director: Edward Rofheart
Publisher: Popular Library
Category: Book

428
Artist: **WILLIAM A. MOTTA**
Category: Editorial

429
Artist: **BERNIE FUCHS**
Art Director: Phil Nash
Client: Carroll & Assoc. Inc.
Category: Advertising

430
Artist: **STEVE KARCHIN**
Art Director: Bill Tidwell
Agency: Doremus & Co.
Client: Atlantic Companies
Category: Institutional

431
Artist: **FRANK WOOTTON**
Art Director: Arnold C. Holeywell
Publisher: Time-Life Books, Inc.
Category: Book

432
Artist: **NICHOLAS SOLOVIOFF**
Art Director: Ronald Campbell
Magazine: Fortune
Category: Editorial

433
Artist: **MITCHELL HOOKS**
Art Director: Soren Noring
Publisher: Reader's Digest
Category: Book

434
Artist: **CHRISTOPHER BLOSSOM**
Art Director: Len Leone
Publisher: Bantam Books
Category: Book

435
Artist: **RON LESSER**
Art Director: Bruce Hall
Publisher: Dell Publishing
Category: Book
Award of Excellence

436
Artist: **BARRON STOREY**
Art Director: Joseph Connolly
Magazine: Boy's Life
Category: Editorial

437
Artist: **WALTER EINSEL**
Client: U.S. Air Force
Category: Institutional

438
Artist: **KEITH FERRIS**
Art Director: Bill Ford
Magazine: Air Force
Category: Institutional

439
Artist: **ALFRED JOHNSON**
Client: Sanders Associates, Inc.
Category: Advertising

440
Artist: **DOUG JOHNSON**
Art Director: Jack Thorwegan
Client: Anheuser-Busch
Category: Institutional

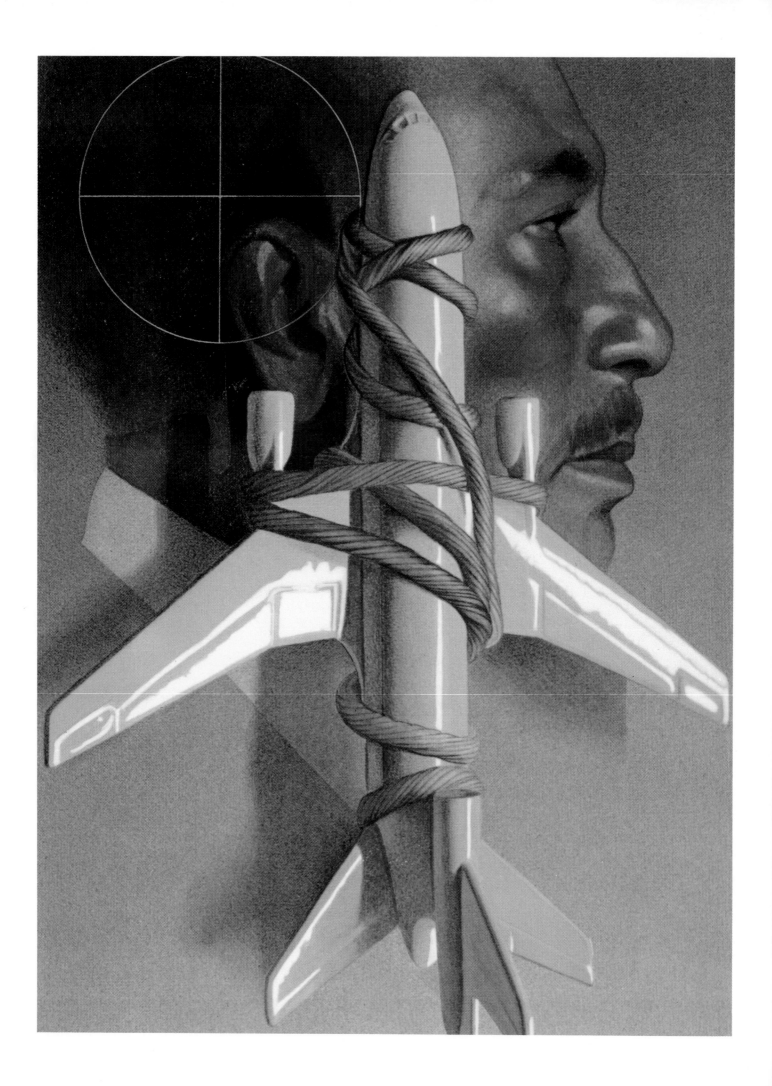

442
Artist: **THOMAS B. ALLEN**
Art Director: Cheryl Tortoriello
Publisher: Prentice Hall
Category: Book

441
Artist: **ALEX GNIDZIEJKO**
Art Director: Joe Brooks
Magazine: Penthouse
Category: Editorial

443
Artist: **RICHARD COURTNEY**
Art Directors: Jim Labbad/Frank Kozelek
Publisher: Berkley Books
Category: Book

444
Artist: **CHARLES SAXON**
Art Director: Linda Stillman
Magazine: Town & Country
Category: Editorial

445
Artist: **EDWARD A. BUTLER**
Art Director: Edward A. Burke
Publisher: John Wiley & Sons
Category: Book

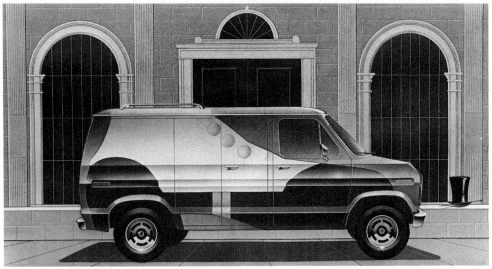

446
Artist: **THEO RUDNAK**
Art Director: George Kubas II
Client: Sherwin Williams Co.
Category: Institutional

447
Artist: **CRAIG TENNANT**
Category: Editorial

448
Artist: **RICHARD KRALL**
Art Director: Dave Shapiro
Agency: Hixo, Inc.
Client: Wheel Records
Category: Advertising
Special Past Chairmen's Committee Award

449
Artist: **CRAIG TENNANT**
Category: Institutional
Award of Excellence

450
Artist: **WILLIAM A. MOTTA**
Art Director: William A. Motta
Magazine: Road & Track
Category: Editorial

451
Artist: **MARK RIEDY**
Category: Editorial

452
Artist: **GARY LUND**
Art Director: Wes Anson
Producer: Lorraine Roberts
Director: Bob Kurtz
Production Company: Kurtz & Friends
Client: Hang Ten International
Category: TV

453
Artist: **BOB ZIERING**
Art Director: Robert Prewett
Client: McCarter Theatre
Category: Advertising

454
Artist: **BOB ZIERING**
Art Directors: Ed Kensinger/Arthur Boden
Client: IBM
Category: Institutional

455
Artist: **TOM YURCICH**
Art Director: Ken Poshedly
Client: American Society for Personnel Administration
Category: Institutional

456
Artist: **JUNE SOBEL**
Art Director: Peter Nevraumont
Client: Ruby Street
Category: Institutional

457
Artist: **DENNIS ZIEMIENSKI**
Client: Paper Moon Graphics Inc.
Category: Institutional

458
Artist: **DENNIS ZIEMIENSKI**
Client: Paper Moon Graphics Inc.
Category: Institutional

459
Artists: **DAVID MYERS/PAMELA NOFTSINGER**
Art Director: Annie Spinelli
Publisher: Dell Publishing
Category: Book

460
Artist: **SUSAN SUMICHRAST**
Art Director: Gordon Mortensen
Magazine: New Realties
Category: Editorial

461
Artists: **MARILYN BASS/MARVIN GOLDMAN**
Art Director: Stanley Wheatman
Publisher: Reader's Digest Educational Division
Category: Book

462
Artist: **BRALDT BRALDS**
Art Director: Richard Aloisio
Magazine: Inside Sports
Category: Editorial

463
Artist: **DAVID GAMBALE**
Category: Institutional

464
Artist: **CAROL WALD**
Art Directors: Kathy Rosenbloom / Judith Fendelman
Publisher: Universe Books
Category: Institutional

465
Artist: **BERNIE FUCHS**
Art Director: Richard Gangel
Magazine: Sports Illustrated
Category: Editorial
Award of Excellence

466
Artist: **HERB TAUSS**
Art Director: Jack Tauss
Publisher: The Franklin Library
Category: Book
Award of Excellence

467
Artist: **RAY DOMINGO**
Art Director: David Bartels
Client: Anheuser-Busch, Inc.
Category: Advertising

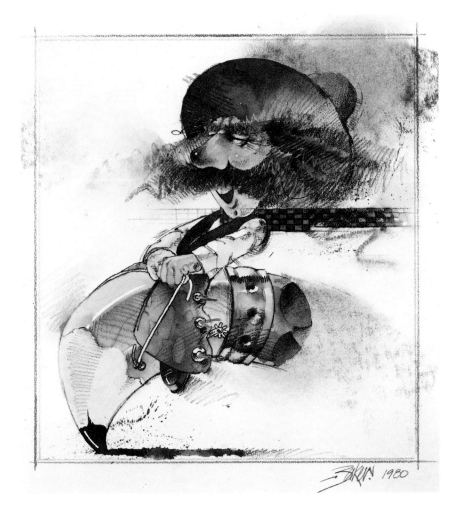

468
Artist: **SCOTT BAKER**
Art Director: Barbara Koster
Magazine: Northwest Orient Airlines "Passages"
Category: Editorial

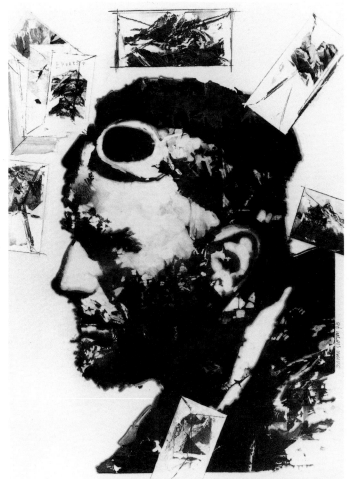

469
Artist: **BARRON STOREY**
Art Director: Noel Werrett
Magazine: Quest/80
Category: Editorial

471
Artist: **WALT SPITZMILLER**
Art Director: Patsy Warner
Client: Manufacturers Hanover Trust
Category: Advertising

470
Artist: **BART FORBES**
Art Directors: Don Baker/Ron Zamorski
Client: Procter & Gamble
Category: Advertising

472
Artist: **DAVID GRIFFIN**
Category: Advertising

473
Artist: **LARRY A. GERBER**
Category: Institutional

474
Artist: **MURRAY TINKELMAN**
Art Director: Milton Charles
Publisher: Pocket Books
Category: Book

475
Artist: **CHARLES SHAW**
Art Director: Jane Palecek
Publisher: Raintree Publishing
Category: Book

476
Artist: **ERALDO CARUGATI**
Art Director: Skip Johnston
Magazine: National Lampoon
Category: Editorial

477
Artist: **ROBERT M. CUNNINGHAM**
Art Director: David G. Foote
Client: U.S. Postal Service
Category: Advertising

478
Artist: **ROBERT M. CUNNINGHAM**
Art Director: David G. Foote
Client: U.S. Postal Service
Category: Institutional

479
Artist: **MILTON GLASER**
Art Director: Milton Glaser
Client: Los Angeles Bicentennial Committee
Category: Advertising
Gold Medal

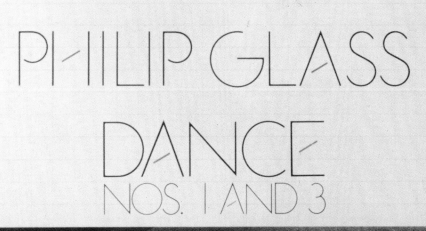

480
Artist: **MILTON GLASER**
Art Director: Milton Glaser
Client: The Tomato Music Company
Category: Advertising

481
Artist: **DAVIS HANNAH**
Art Director: Gerry Contreras
Client: R.S.V.P.
Category: Institutional

482
Artist: **ROBERT M. CUNNINGHAM**
Art Director: David G. Foote
Client: U.S. Postal Service
Category: Institutional

483
Artist: **MILAN KECMAN**
Publication: The Cleveland Plain Dealer Magazine
Category: Editorial

484
Artist: **RICH GROTE**
Art Director: Charles Kornberger
Agency: Benton & Bowles
Client: Milliken Visa
Category: Advertising

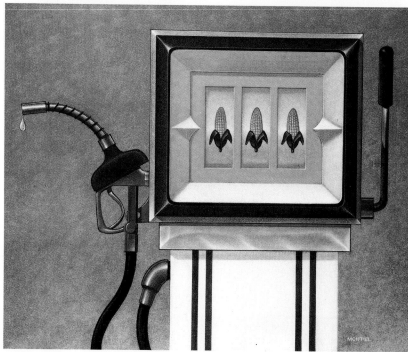

485
Artist: **DAVID MONTIEL**
Art Director: Lester Goodman
Client: Next Magazine
Category: Television

486
Artist: **RAY AMEIJIDE**
Art Director: Roy Cherwin
Agency: Cannon Adv. Inc.
Client: Las Hadas-Mexico
Category: Advertising

487
Artist: **JÖZEF SUMICHRAST**
Art Director: Bernie Colonna
Client: American Express
Category: Institutional

488
Artist: **PAT NAGEL**
Art Director: Louise Kollenbaum
Magazine: Mother Jones
Category: Editorial

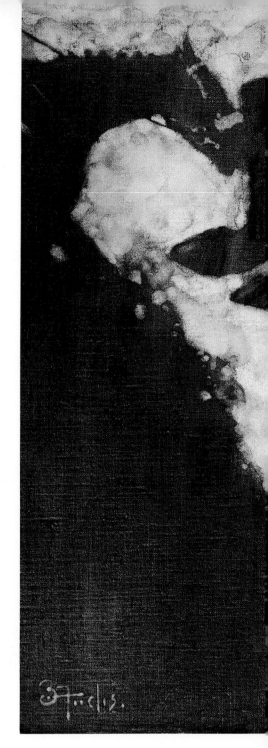

489
Artist: **JACK PARDUE**
Art Director: Alan Forquer
Publisher: Review & Herald Publishing Co.
Category: Book

490
Artist: **BERNIE FUCHS**
Art Director: William Gregory
Publisher: Reader's Digest
Category: Book

491
Artist: **BERNIE FUCHS**
Art Directors: Ken Ellis/Marion Davis
Publisher: Reader's Digest
Category: Book

492
Artist: **DICKRAN PALULIAN**
Art Director: Lester Goodman
Magazine: Next
Category: Editorial

493
Artist: **ERHARD GOTTLICHER**
Art Directors: Werner Kustermann / William Gregory
Publisher: Reader's Digest
Category: Book

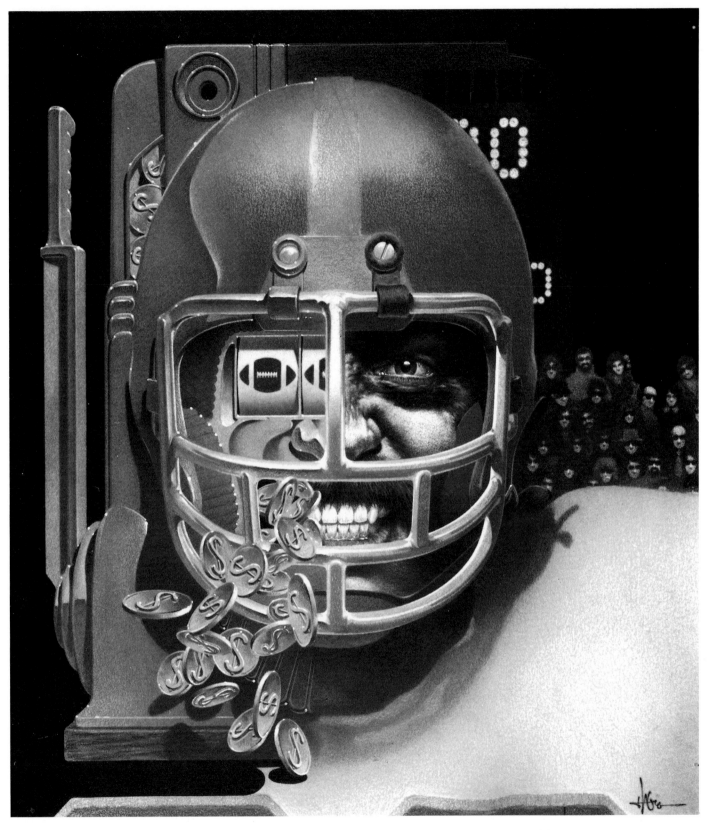

494
Artist: **KUNIO HAGIO**
Art Directors: Tom Staebler/Kerig Pope
Magazine: Playboy
Category: Editorial
Award of Excellence

495
Artist: **BART FORBES**
Art Director: Richard Gangel
Magazine: Sports Illustrated
Category: Editorial

496
Artist: **BART FORBES**
Art Director: David Boss
Client: NFL Properties
Category: Institutional

497
Artist: **DON DAILY**
Art Directors: Gerald Counihan/Edward Rofheart
Publisher: Fawcett Books
Category: Book

498
Artist: **GILLIAN HILLS**
Art Director: Milton Charles
Publisher: Pocket Books
Category: Book

499
Artist: **BILL GREER**
Art Director: Barbara Bertoli
Publisher: Avon Books
Category: Book

500
Artist: **JEAN LEON HUENS**
Art Director: J. Robert Terringo
Magazine: National Geographic
Category: Editorial

502
Artist: **DON WELLER**
Art Director: Greg Wilder
Client: Sun Graphics
Category: Institutional

501
Artist: **BOB DACEY**
Art Director: Pete Libby
Magazine: Golf Digest
Category: Editorial
Gold Medal

503
Artist: **WILLIAM HARMUTH**
Art Director: Jack Tauss
Publisher: The Franklin Library
Category: Book

504
Artist: **JACK ENDEWELT**
Art Director: Jack Tauss
Publisher: The Franklin Library
Category: Book

505
Artist: **WILSON McLEAN**
Art Director: Joe Brooks
Magazine: Penthouse
Category: Editorial

506
Artist: **JAMES McMULLAN**
Art Director: Johnny Lee
Client: Elektra/Asylum/Nonesuch
Category: Advertising

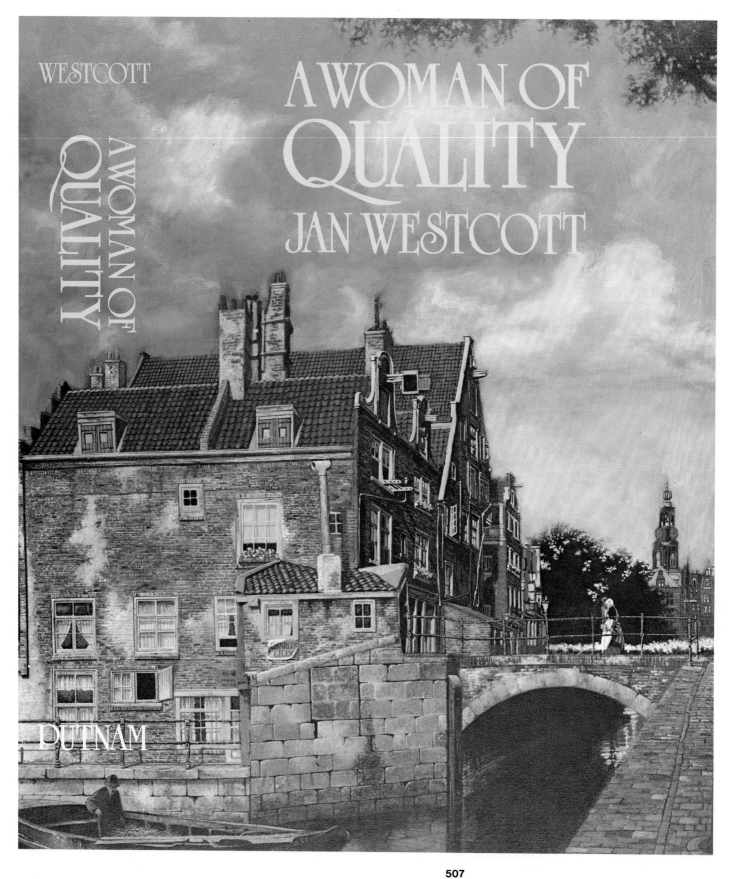

WESTCOTT

A WOMAN OF QUALITY

JAN WESTCOTT

A WOMAN OF QUALITY

PUTNAM

507
Artist: **CHARLES LILLY**
Art Director: Lynn Hollyn
Publisher: G.P. Putnam
Category: Book

508
Artist: **RICHARD SPARKS**
Art Director: Tom Lulovitch
Magazine: U.S. Air "Inflight"
Category: Editorial

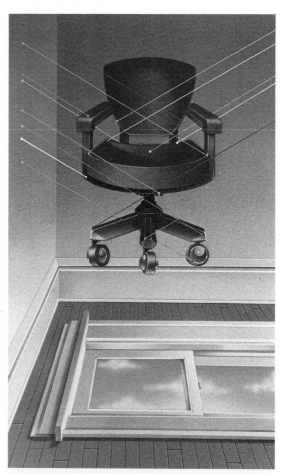

509
Artist: **THEO RUDNAK**
Art Director: Marlene Rudnak
Category: Institutional

510
Artist: **ANDREW GASKILL**
Category: Institutional

511
Artist: **ERHARD GOTTLICHER**
Art Directors: Werner Kustermann/William Gregory
Publisher: Reader's Digest
Category: Book

512
Artist: **CHRIS VAN ALLSBURG**
Art Director: Walter Lorraine
Publisher: Houghton Mifflin
Category: Book

513
Artist: **CRAIG NELSON**
Art Director: June Dutton
Client: Determined Productions, Inc.
Category: Book
Award of Excellence

514
Artist: **JAMES C. REYMAN**
Client: Parsons School of Design
Category: Editorial

515
Artist: **GEORGE PORTER**
Client: Walter R. Heed
Category: Editorial

516
Artist: **JOHN JUDE PALENCAR**
Art Director: Larry Bode
Client: Columbus College of Art and Design
Category: Advertising

517
Artist: **ROGER KASTEL**
Art Director: Milton Charles
Publisher: Pocket Books
Category: Book

Two of the hottest book titles this Christmas gift season are *The Westing Game* by Ellen Raskin and *The Girl Who Loved Wild Horses* by Paul Goble. If they don't sound familiar, aren't as immediately recognizable as, say, *Sophie's Choice* or *Jailbird*, it may be simply that you're on the wrong side of the generation gap.

For, as every child and children's book-buying parent knows, *The Westing Game* and *The Girl Who Loved Wild Horses* are this year's winners, respectively, of the Newbery and Caldecott Medals, the Oscars of children's literature. The American Library Association (ALA) has been presenting the Newbery, named for the eighteenth-century British writer considered the father of modern English-language children's books, every year since 1922 for "the most distinguished contribution to children's literature." The Caldecott, instituted in 1938 and named for the classic English artist Randolph Caldecott, is given for "the most distinguished picture book." The ALA will meet in Chicago next month to name the winners who will reap their rewards next Christmas (and for many Christmases to come).

The payoff can be considerable. Although the immediate dollars may not be in league with adult best-sellers, the long-term profits from a Newbery or Caldecott can far exceed the possibilities of any single title in the adult book trade. Such an award assures a book's sales for generations; a brisk business is still being done in such prize titles as

THE CHILDREN'S HOUR See the new Dick. See the new Jane. See them laugh. See them laugh all the way to the bank
BY JEAN F. MERCIER

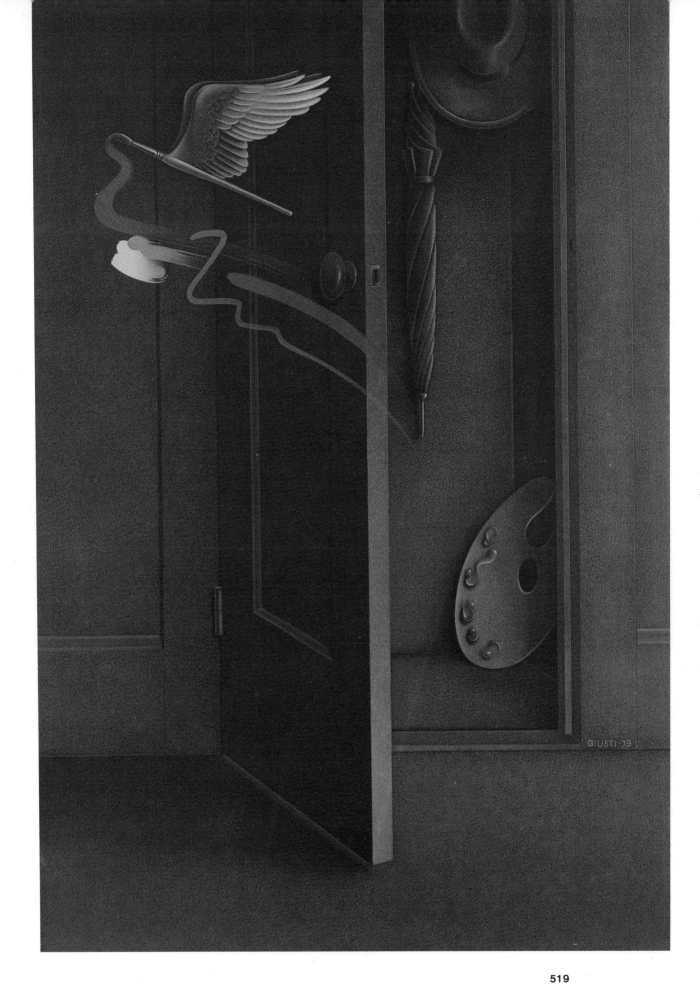

518
Artist: **JOHN CRAIG**
Art Director: Alfred Zelcer
Magazine: TWA Ambassador
Category: Editorial

519
Artist: **ROBERT GIUSTI**
Art Director: Silas Rhodes
Client: School of Visual Arts
Category: Institutional
Award of Excellence

520
Artist: **JOSEPH CIARDIELLO**
Art Director: Richard Aloisio
Magazine: Inside Sports
Category: Editorial

521
Artist: **CHRISTOPHER BARTLETT**
Art Director: Christopher Bartlett
Client: Towson State University
Category: Institutional

THE FINAL LUNCHEON OF THE EARL OF SANDWICH
PLATE NO. 43

522
Artist: **TIM RAGLIN**
Art Director: Noel Werrett
Magazine: Quest/80
Category: Editorial

523
Artist: **LISBETH ZWERGER**
Art Director: Michael Neugebauer
Publisher: Morrow Junior Books
Category: Book

524
Artist: **LISBETH ZWERGER**
Art Director: Michael Neugebauer
Publisher: Morrow Junior Books
Category: Book

525
Artist: **LISBETH ZWERGER**
Art Director: Michael Neugebauer
Publisher: Morrow Junior Books
Category: Book

526
Artist: **BILL CIGLIANO**
Category: Book

527
Artist: **JACK ENDEWELT**
Category: Advertising

528
Artist: **ROGER HUYSSEN**
Art Director: Bob Defrin
Client: Atlantic Records
Category: Advertising

529
Artist: **REYNOLD RUFFINS**
Art Director: Bo Costello
Agency: Willis, Case, Harwood Inc.
Client: Mead Paper
Category: Institutional
Award of Excellence

530
Artist: **DON WELLER**
Art Director: Cliff Wynne
Magazine: Playgirl
Category: Editorial

531
Artist: **DEBBIE KUHN**
Art Director: Frank Rizzo
Agency: Tracy Locke Advertising
Client: Phillips 66
Category: Advertising

532
Artist: **JOZEF SUMICHRAST**
Art Directors: Don Duffy/Don Hedin
Publication: Reader's Digest
Category: Editorial

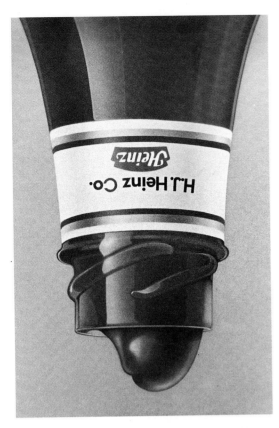

533
Artist: **THEO RUDNAK**
Art Director: Dan Sell
Client: Sell Inc.
Category: Advertising

534
Artist: **JACK ENDEWELT**
Category: Editorial

535
Artist: **BOB PEPPER**
Art Director: Fred Martin
Agency: Robert A. Becker Inc.
Client: Mead-Johnson Pharmaceutical Division
Category: Advertising

536
Artist: **ROSEKRANS HOFFMAN**
Art Director: Kathleen Tucker
Publisher: Albert Whitman & Co.
Category: Book

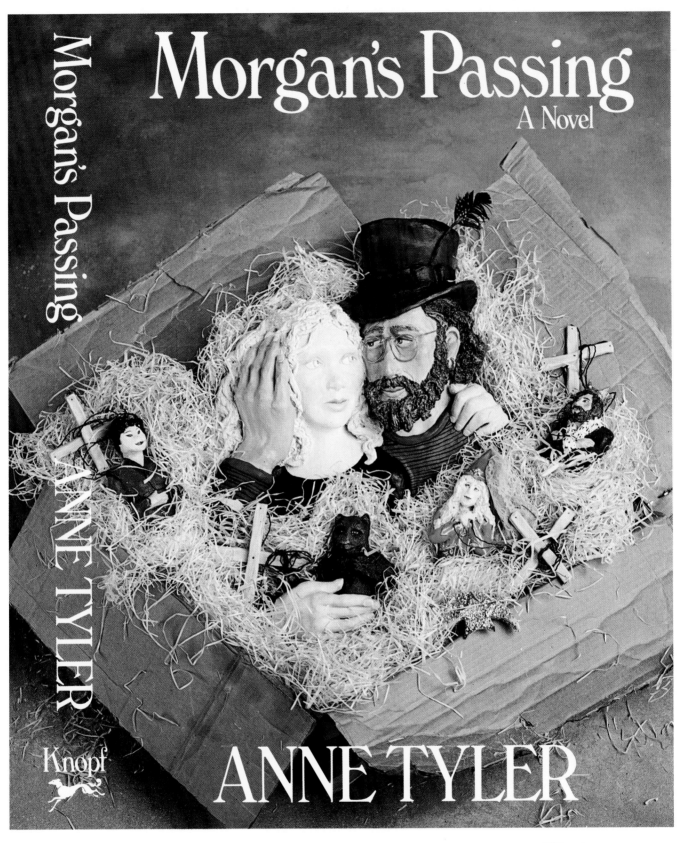

Morgan's Passing

Morgan's Passing
A Novel
ANNE TYLER

ANNE TYLER

Knopf

537
Artist: **BROOKIE MAXWELL**
Art Director: Betty Anderson
Publisher: Alfred A. Knopf Inc.
Category: Book

538
Artist: **ERIC FOWLER**
Category: Institutional

539
Artist: **CATHY BARANCIK**
Art Director: Don Freidman
Cleint: Pinky & Dianne
Category: Advertising

540
Artist: **JANET MAGER**
Art Director: Gill Fishman
Client: Rainboworld
Category: Institutional

541
Artist: **MARGARET CUSACK**
Art Director: Robert Glassman
Client: D.P.F., Inc.
Category: Institutional

Margaret's death was an awakening

Margaret Redmond died at 16, haunted by a guilty passion. Now she awoke in a place whose peace and serenity she somehow remembered. And there she found Paul, the beautiful young man she knew she had loved before. With Paul to guide her, Margaret embarked on a strange and wondrous journey through timeless reaches of the human soul... to a final heart's awakening.

Song of the Pearl A mystic idyll of eternal love and of lovers forever bound.

BANTAM BOOKS

FANTASY
$1.75

11662-2 ★ $1.75 ★ A BANTAM BOOK ®

Song of the Pearl·Ruth Nichols

0-553-
11662-2

A fantasy of eternal love in a land beyond this life

Song of the Pearl
by Ruth Nichols

542
Artist: **ELIZABETH MALCZYNSKI**
Art Director: Len Leone
Publisher: Bantam Books
Category: Book

543
Artists: **LEO & DIANE DILLON**
Art Director: Barbara G. Hennessy
Publisher: Viking Penguin Inc.
Category: Book

544 *Japan*
Artist: **SHIGEO OKAMOTO**
Client: Seibu-Kasugai
Category: Advertising

FOREIGN ILLUSTRATION

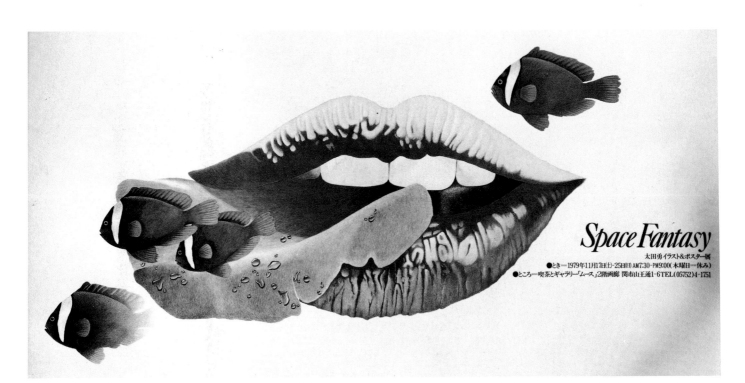

545 *Japan*
Artist: **ISAMU OHTA**
Client: Gallery Moose, Shingifu Department Store Co. Ltd.
Category: Advertising

546 *Spain*
Artist: **RAMON GONZALEZ TEJA**
Client: Lui (España)
Category: Editorial

547   *Japan*
Artist: **KEIICHI MURAKAMI**
Publisher: Seitôsha Inc.
Category: Book
Award of Excellence

548   *Japan*
Artist: **SHUZO KATO**
Client: Yamaha
Category: Advertising

549 *Japan*
Artist: **SAEKO TSUEMURA**
Category: Editorial

550 *Japan*
Artist: **YOSHIRO KATO**
Category: Institutional

551 *Mexico*
Artist: **SERGIO MARTINEZ**
Category: Institutional

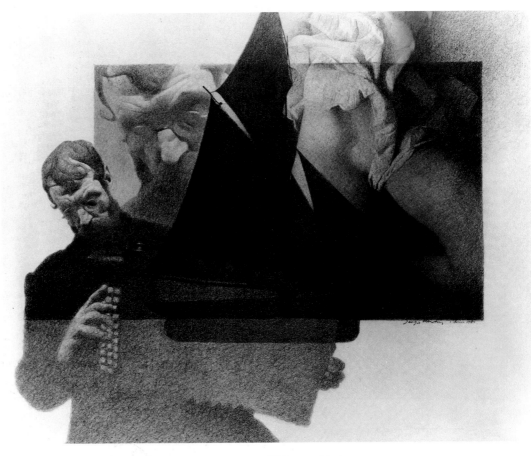

552 *Mexico*
Artist: **SERGIO MARTINEZ**
Category: Institutional

553 *Mexico*
Artist: **SERGIO MARTINEZ**
Category: Institutional

554 *Canada*
Artist: **JAMES HILL**
Art Director: Margaret Stewart
Magazine: Imperial Oil Ltd's ''The Review''
Category: Editorial

555 *Japan*
Artist: **TOSHIKANE TANAKA**
Category: Advertising

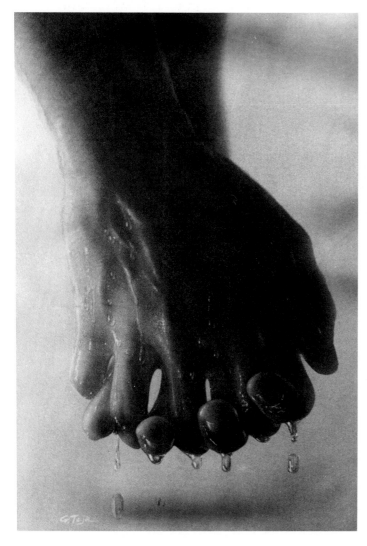

556 *Spain*
Artist: **RAMON GONZALEZ TEJA**
Publication: El Pais
Category: Editorial

557 *Japan*
Artist: **HIDEAKI KODAMA**
Category: Editorial

宇宙科学をめぐる九つの対談 対話 宇宙探訪 荒 正人 編◯講談社◯520円
BLUE·BACKS

558 *Japan*
Artist: **EIKO KAJIURA**
Category: Editorial

559 *Germany*
Artist: **RI KAISER**
Art Director: M. Wessel
Client: Miller-International
Category: Advertising

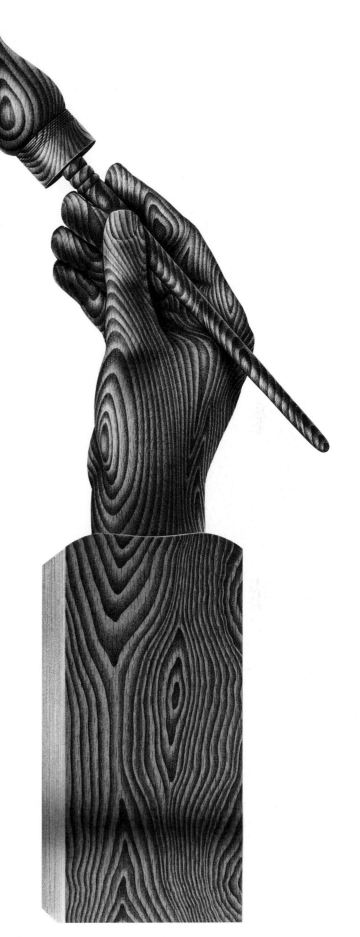

560 *Germany*
Artist: **RI KAISER**
Art Director: Walther Weiss
Client: GGK Advertising Agency
Category: Advertising

561   *Brazil*
Artist: **OSWALDO MIRANDA**
Publication: Newspaper Diário do Paraná
Category: Editorial

562   *Brazil*
Artist: **OSWALDO MIRANDA**
Publication: Newspaper Diario do Paraná
Category: Editorial

563   *Canada*
Artist: **JEFF JACKSON**
Art Director: Derick Ungless
Magazine: Saturday Night
Category: Editorial

564 *Brazil*
Artist: **OSWALDO MIRANDA**
Client: Gravartex Photolletering
Category: Institutional

565 *Brazil*
Artist: **OSWALDO MIRANDA**
Client: Gravartex Photolletering
Category: Institutional

566 *Canada*
Artist: **JEFF JACKSON**
Art Director: Louis Fishauf
Magazine: Toronto Star's City
Category: Editorial

567 *Japan*
Artist: **TSUTOMU HOKAZONO**
Publisher: Flureberukan Co. Ltd.
Category: Book

568 *Australia*
Artist: **BRIAN CLINTON**
Art Director: Steve Bowman
Client: Australian Tourist Commission
Category: Advertising

569 *Japan*
Artist: **KENJI NOTO**
Category: Institutional
Award of Excellence

水と緑の豊かな環境を！
自然環境を見守る会

570 *Canada*
Artist: **TINA HOLDCROFT**
Art Director: Margaret Stewart
Magazine: Imperial Oil Ltd's ''The Review''
Category: Editorial

571 *Canada*
Artist: **MYRA LOWENTHAL**
Category: Editorial

572 *Canada*
Artist: **MYRA LOWENTHAL**
Category: Editorial

573 *Spain*
Artist: **RAMON GONZALEZ TEJA**
Client: Lui (España)
Category: Editorial

574 *Canada*
Artist: **MYRA LOWENTHAL**
Category: Editorial

575 *Japan*
Artist: **KAZUO YAMAMOTO**
Client: Graphic Ad
Category: Advertising

576 *Japan*
Artist: **KAZUMASA TSUIHIJI**
Category: Institutional

577 *Japan*
Artist: **NOBUTSUNA WATANABE**
Category: Book

578 *Japan*
Artist: **SHUN ISHIKAWA**
Art Director: Hiroshi Morishima
Client: Nomura Display Co., Ltd.
Category: Advertising

579 *Spain*
Artist: **JAVIER ROMERO**
Publication: El Pais
Category: Editorial

580 *Japan*
Artist: **KEIJI SUGITA**
Art Director: Takayoshi Kato
Agency: Meitetu Advertising Inc.
Client: Japan National Railways
Category: Advertising

581 *Japan*
Artist: **KATSUHIKO IKEDA**
Category: Advertising

582 *Canada*
Artist: **MURIEL WOOD**
Art Director: Margaret Stewart
Magazine: Imperial Oil Ltd's "The Review"
Category: Editorial

583 *Canada*
Artist: **MURIEL WOOD**
Art Director: Bob Young
Publisher: McLelland & Stewart
Category: Book

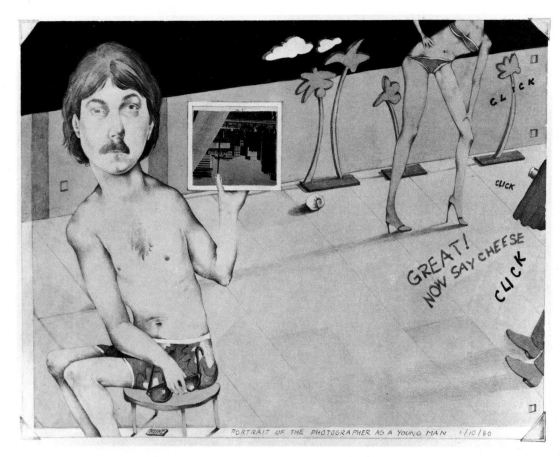

584   *Canada*
Artist: **ANITA KUNZ**
Category: Editorial

585   *Canada*
Artist: **ANITA KUNZ**
Category: Editorial

586   *Canada*
Artist: **JOHN MARTIN**
Art Director: Jackie Young
Magazine: Financial Post
Category: Editorial

587 *Spain*
Artist: **RAMON GONZALEZ TEJA**
Client: The Illustrators Workshop
Category: Editorial

588 *Canada*
Artist: **DAVID J. BATHURST**
Category: Editorial

589 *France*
Artist: **MICHEL GUIRÉ-VAKA**
Category: Editorial

590 *France*
Artist: **MICHEL GUIRÉ-VAKA**
Category: Editorial

591 *Canada*
Artist: **JOHN MARTIN**
Art Director: Andrew Smith
Magazine: Graduate
Category: Editorial

INDEX

INDEX

ARTISTS

FOREIGN ILLUSTRATORS

ART DIRECTORS

FILM DIRECTORS

FILM PRODUCERS

Ongoing projects conceived and administered by the members and staff of the Society of Illustrators.

The New Gallery

This is how MUSEUM MAGAZINE reviewed the Society of Illustrators new Gallery:

"The Society, a New York landmark since 1901, has recently expanded and has opened the new Museum of American Illustration. This extra space permits the Society to increase its exhibition schedule. It now has the capacity to present an exhibition of large scope, or two smaller ones simultaneously.

The Society has a superb collection of historical and contemporary illustration, work by artists at the forefront of their profession. It is deeply involved in the education and training of young artists who want to enter the field."

The expanded gallery space was made possible by the contributions from Society members and a generous donation by J. Walter Thompson Co.

The Permanent Collection now contains over 800 individual works ranging from a Rockwell to a recent Bob Peak.

The Society with its new Museum will now be able to properly house its growing collection of past and contemporary illustration.

The members of the first Museum Committee are: Art Weithas, Dir.; John Moodie, Permanent Collection Ch.; Howard Munce, Walt Reed, Murray Tinkelman; and Terrence Brown, Curator.

The Annual Show

Each April the Past Chairmen's Committee meets to ignite the forthcoming show, and the sparks begin to fly. A designer is selected for the "Call for Entries" poster and lists of nine jurors for each category are compiled.

Much consideration is given to forming well balanced juries; a diverse blend of art directors and illustrators representing a wide range of styles, tastes and viewpoints are selected. A limited number of Society members are included.

Next, the staff takes over and the nitty-gritty begins. Entries pour in — right up until the October deadline. The juries then meet to review each of the thousands of entries submitted to select those for inclusion in the show and for the granting of awards.

In January, approximately 500 selected originals arrive from all parts of the country, they are hung in the Society's gallery in two phases — each on exhibit for one month. The flow of traffic is unending and overwhelming — but the response from the thousands who come is so gratifying that the months of effort are made worthwhile.

The circle is complete. The show has ended. It's April again.

If you wish your name added to this Call for Entries list write for: The Annual Exhibition "Call for Entries."

The Student Scholarship Competition

Since its inception in 1962, the Society's Annual Student Exhibition has grown steadily in size and importance, giving young illustrators a much sought-after opportunity to display their work before an audience of art directors, buyers, representatives, established illustrators and the general public.

Each fall the Society sends out a "Call for Entries" to approximately 1,000 art schools and universities nationwide. Students submit work done the preceding year. A panel of jurors selects between 150-175 of the best to be exhibited in the spring in the Society's Museum. Out of this collection, about 30 of the most outstanding are selected as the award winners. Thousands of dollars in cash prizes are granted. All students in the show receive a Certificate of Merit.

The quality of work in recent years has been so skillful, innovative and exciting that the Society's Board of Directors voted to record the exhibitions in catalogue form. Every piece in the show is reproduced in the catalogue, along with credits for students, instructors and schools.

This combination of exhibition and catalogue gives students an exposure to the professional world that they would otherwise never receive. The Society is proud to sponsor this annual competition.

Open to college level illustration students, the competition must be entered *through schools only*, not by individual students. If you wish to enter this competition, ask your instructor to write for: The Student Competition "Call for Entries."

Our Own Publications

ILLUSTRATION IN THE THIRD DIMENSION

Volume 1 in the *Society of Illustrators Library of American Illustration*

A selection of ingenious and original dimensional work by leading illustrators and designers turned craftsmen who have freed themselves of the limits of the flat surface to solve a wide range of assignments. Each illustrator discloses tips on the methods and materials which include everything from lobster traps to rusted cans to shirt buttons.

MAGIC AND OTHER REALISM

Volume 2 in the *Society of Illustrators Library of American Illustration*

A cross section of work by leading illustrators in the field of "realistic" painting and drawing. The book dramatically displays the way in which artists heighten and stretch the realistic aspects of their work to increase the impact of the final image. Each contributor discusses the philosophies, methods and materials used in creating this special, precise and painstaking kind of illustration.

To order either of the above send $16.50 per book, plus $2.00 postage for each.

TWENTY YEARS OF AWARD WINNERS

Each year out of the 500 plus illustrations the juries accept for the Society of Illustrators Annual Exhibition, a few are singled out to receive the coveted Gold Medal or Award of Excellence. This volume which includes a brief history of illustration and a discussion of its future, is devoted to those award winners from 1959-1970, the first two decades of the publication of the Illustrators Annual. This volume contains 112 works in full color.

To order, send $59.95 plus $3.00 postage.

Address all inquiries and requests for specific books and entry forms to

Society of Illustrators

128 East 63rd Street
New York, N.Y. 10021
212-838-2560

How do gold medal winners begin their Illustration Careers?

NINETEEN HUNDRED EIGHTY-ONE
SCHOOL OF VISUAL ARTS
ILLUSTRATION PORTFOLIO

The major objective of the Media Department at the School of Visual Arts is to educate artists who can continue to believe in their possibilities for personal expression while producing art to meet the minds and needs of other people.

The Illustration major faces the reality of freelance illustration immediately after graduation. Not only must he or she find work in the marketplace, but there is the pressure of knowing that the work will be judged by standards of professional excellence. The portfolio of work reproduced on these pages can meet those standards. The selection was made by a jury of four exceptional art directors working in New York City. Bob Ciano, Art Director, Life Magazine; Bob Defrin, Art Director, Atlantic Records; Frank Devino, Art Director, Omni Magazine and Mary Shanahan, Art Director, Rolling Stone Magazine.

Each of them is committed to the use of quality illustration and despite hectic schedules make time to review new work from all over the country.

I would like to thank them for the many long hours spent considering each piece submitted, for making the difficult decisions that resulted in this final selection of work reproduced here. Their choices reflect the wide range of expression representing the class of June, 1981.

My thanks, also, to David Rhodes, the President of the School of Visual Arts, for his continuing support and enthusiasm for this project.

Marshall Arisman

Marshall Arisman, Co-Chairman, Media Arts Department, Head of Illustration

Visual Arts believes talent deserves first class presentation. See it for yourselves. The portfolio contains 72 pages, 8½" x 11", handsomely bound and printed in full color. A free personal copy of this exciting student work is waiting for you. Send now. Supply is limited. Call or write Eileen McClash, Placement Director, The School of Visual Arts, 209 East 23rd Street, New York, New York 10010.

SCHOOL OF
VISUAL ARTS

John Rush

The Little Browne Book

David Plourde

Paul Reott

George Angelini

Ted Enik

Ron Jones

Joe Burleson

Glee LoScalzo

pema browne ltd. /369-1925

185 east 85th st., new york, 10028

Illustration and Literary Agents

PEMA BROWNE

PERRY J. BROWNE

Tom Leonard

KIRCHOFF/WOHLBERG, INC
ARTISTS REPRESENTATIVE

433 East 51 Street, New York, N.Y. 10022   212 • 753 • 5146
897 Boston Post Road, Madison, Ct. 06443   203 • 245 • 7308

artists

Norman Adams, Don Brautigam,
Michael Deas, Alex Gnidziejko,
Robert Heindel, Steve Karchin,
Dick Krepel, Skip Liepke,
Rick McCollum, Fred Otnes,
Hodges Soileau

Represented by:
Bill Erlacher, Artists Associates
211 East 51 Street, New York, N.Y. 10022
Telephone: (212) 755-1365/6
Associate: Nicole Edell

joann daley

joann daley

joann daley

john robinette

john robinette

bruce emmett

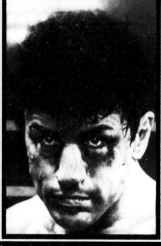

kunio hagio

kunio hagio

MOTION PICTURE ADVERTISING ONLY AND ON THE WEST COAST.

kunio hagio

pat dunn

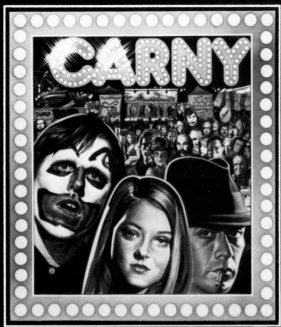
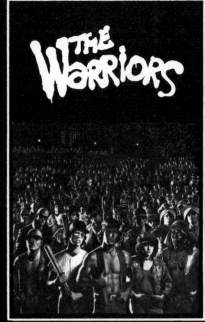

david jarvis   **david jarvis**   **david jarvis**

eraldo carugati in association with   **bart forbes**   **bart forbes**

WEST COAST ONLY.

STEPHENS BIONDI DeCICCO INC.

dennis magdich   **jack thurston**

WEST COAST ONLY.

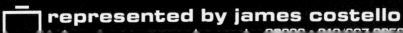

represented by james costello

ARE YOU A POTENTIAL SUPERSTAR

?

Isn't it about time you found out? Syracuse University's Independent Study Degree Program gives you an opportunity to work toward your MFA in Advertising Design or Illustration while you're working full time. And you study face-to-face with the top designers and illustrators in the industry.

For two weeks each summer (for three summers) you study with superstars like the former faculty listed below. The rest of the year you're working on independent study assignments and making a few long-weekend field trips to study with the top communicators right where they live and work. Places like New York,

Toronto, Chicago and London.

You'll find out more about how the pros work, you'll make more connections and you'll learn more than you can possibly imagine.

For information contact: Director, Syracuse University ISDP / **Room 45.** 610 E. Fayette Street / Syracuse, N.Y. 13202 / (315) 423-3269.

Study with the pros ALLAN BEAVER, JOE BOWLER, TOM CARNASE, MILTON CHARLES, STEVE COSMOPULOS, PAUL DAVIS, LOU DORFSMAN, GENE FEDERICO, DICK GANGEL, AMIL GARGANO, BOB GROSSMAN, DICK HARVEY, BOB HEINDEL, DOUG JOHNSON, DICK HESS, HELMUT KRONE, HERB LUBALIN, WILSON McCLEAN, JIM McMULLAN, JACQUI MORGAN, DAVE PASSALACQUA, ARTHUR PAUL, LARRY PLAPLER, SHIRLEY POLYKOFF, HEIDI RICKABAUGH, SAM SCALI, EILEEN HEDY SCHULTZ, ISADORE SELTZER, BERT STEINHAUSER, MURRAY TINKELMAN, DON TROUSDELL & ROBERT WEAVER

OUR TEN COMMANDMENTS of ARTIST REPRESENTATION

1. We represent only artists we believe in and are totally committed to them.

2. We believe in being more than agents and become involved in the *total career* of the artists we represent.

3. We appreciate the problems of the artist and try, whenever possible, to alleviate these problems.

4. We also appreciate the problems of the art director: his client-agency relationship, tight deadlines and budget limitations and try to help him solve these problems whenever we can.

5. We believe in *full representation.* That means taking on only that number of artists that we can fully represent as well as insuring that each artist is non-competitive in style with other artists we represent.

6. We believe in giving *full service* to our artists and to the art director, promptly and professionally. Every client, no matter what the job price, deserves the very best we can offer.

7. We believe in being *flexible.* Business conditions change. The economy rises and falls. Accounts switch. We and our artists must adjust to all changes in order to successfully survive.

8. We believe in always meeting deadlines and always keeping a bargain. We and our artists are only as good as our word and our last job.

9. We believe in *BEING HONEST* at all times. With our artists. With the art director. With ourselves.

10. And finally, we believe in our *profession...* the profession of representing artists. We firmly believe that it is the most exciting and challenging profession anywhere and we are proud to be a part of it.

Barbara Gordon
Associates Ltd.
165 East 32 Street
New York, N.Y. 10016
212-686-3514

Designed by Kumquat Productions Photo by Jim Houghton

Koh-I-Noor is offering for $35 each
a limited edition of lithograph prints
of this drawing by Ruth Daniels. The
prints, on fine quality white stock,
22″ x 28″ (image 14½″ x 19″), are
reproduced from the original artwork
now in the Koh-I-Noor Permanent Collection.
Individually signed by the artist. Print only.
Please allow three to four weeks for delivery.
Send the coupon.

RAPIDOGRAPH® ART

. . . the horses of Ruth Daniels

accomplished by modeling supple textures with a fine stippling technique, laying in darker planes among the highlights. The many hours devoted to this achievement required the dependability and consistent ink flow made possible in part by a patented DRY DOUBLE-SEAL™ cap liner which provides airtight seals for instant startup and optimum drawing time. It is this kind of dependability that makes the Rapidograph the most widely used technical pen in the United States and Canada.

For your best effort in pen-and-ink drawing, be sure the pen is Rapidograph. It makes a difference if you want to achieve the precision and definition of ink lines Koh-I-Noor has made possible through constant research and development since introducing the first technical pen in 1954. It makes a difference, if you want to master the inked values that created the gentle equine eyes of artist Daniels' horses.

"Get-acquainted packaging" (product number 3165-BX) offers a special savings with a pen-and-ink combination. Ask your dealer, or send the coupon for details.

Ruth C. Daniels

KOH-I-NOOR
RAPIDOGRAPH®

☐ Please send me your complimentary Catalog E describing Rapidograph Technical Pens, point sizes, Koh-I-Noor and Pelikan inks and other artist materials.

☐ Please send me the names of Koh-I-Noor dealers in my area.

☐ Please find enclosed my check or money order for $ _____ to cover _____ Horses of Ruth Daniels print(s) at $35.00 (U.S.) per print, which includes handling and shipping.

Name (please print or type)

Company Name if the following is a business address

No. and Street

City   State   Zip

Koh-I-Noor Rapidograph, Inc.   In Canada: 1815 Meyerside Dr.
Bloomsbury, N.J. 08804   Mississauga, Ont. L5T 1B4
(201) 479-4124   (416) 671-0696

® RAPIDOGRAPH is a Registered Trademark of Koh-I-Noor Rapidograph, Inc.

Illustrations by the
artist: Raymond Kursar

To view Portfolio or to arrange for Slide Presentation
Call or write to Raymond Kursar—One Lincoln Plaza
New York, N.Y. 10023 (212) 873-5605

Dell Publishing/Reader's Digest/Zebra Books/Grossett & Dunlap/Ace/Hearst Publications/Avon

See former ads in Illustrators Annuals 15, 18, 19, 20, 21, 22

Harvey Kahn's newest associate is Douglas Kahn.

Harvey Kahn Associates, Inc.
70 E. 56st. New York, New York 10022   212-752-8490